Christmas Angels
All Year Round

Angels
We Have Heard
on High

Angels
We Have Heard
on High

A Book of Seasonal Blessings

JOAN WESTER ANDERSON

CARMEL • NEW YORK 10512

This Guideposts edition is published by special arrangement with Ballantine Books.

LIBRARY OF CONGRESS CATALOGING-IN-PUBLICATION DATA

Anderson, Joan Wester.
  Angels we have heard on high : a book of seasonal blessings /
Joan Wester Anderson.—1st ed.
    p.   cm.
  Includes bibliographical references.
  ISBN 0-345-41203-6 (hc: alk. paper)
    1. Christian life—Fiction.   2. Christmas stories.   I. Title.
  BV4515.2.A49   197   97-20969
  242'.335—dc21

http://www.guideposts.org
Design by José R. Fonfrias
Typeset by Composition Technologies, Inc.
Manufactured in the United States of America

The Lord bless you and keep you.
The Lord let his face shine upon you,
and be gracious to you.
The Lord look upon you kindly and
give you peace.

—Numbers 6:24–26

⮑ Contents ⮐

INTRODUCTION   3

Upon a Midnight Clear   6

With Songs of Rejoicing   11

Any Caring Person   14

Oh, Holy Night   18

The Light of Love   25

Angels We Have Heard (and Seen) on High   30

The Visitor   36

All Ye Faithful   41

Hope Is Where the Heart Is   46

The Power of Prayer   51

The Ten Percent Solution   57

Contents

A Mother's Job   62

That's What Friends Are For   67

Over the Hills, and Everywhere   72

NOTES   77

AFTERWORD   79

Angels
We Have Heard
on High

Introduction

I am the servant of the Lord. Let it be
done to me as you say.

—LUKE 1:38

HEY WERE YOUNG NEWLYWEDS on a difficult journey to a country where they had never been before. They had no hotel reservations, friends, or hearty bank balance to sustain them now or when they arrived. To make matters worse, she was pregnant and close to her time of delivery. But the baby was not her husband's child. It had been conceived during their engagement period, in a way she still could not fully explain. She had felt certain he would abandon her once he learned of the new life within her. What man wouldn't feel betrayed, stricken with sorrow and anger as the life they'd so lovingly planned together came crashing down at his feet? And yet, when Heaven asked her if she would accept this precious assignment and carry it out on faith—with no guarantees other than that God would be with her through it all—she had risked everything and agreed.

Her fiance had not deserted her, after all. Hurt and confused, he had considered it. But he loved her, and although his confidence in her was shaken, he couldn't escape the notion that, despite appearances, there had to be a reasonable explanation for what she had done. Then one night an angel had visited him in a dream, and told him to trust, that there was nothing to worry about, that all would be revealed in due time. And on this shakiest of evidence, in a leap of faith that rivaled her own, the young man had married her.

Despite their precarious beginning and uncertain circumstances, they were both aware that their unborn child was even more vulnerable than their marriage. He depended upon them for His very survival. Their primary job during these coming years would be to give life to Him, nurture Him, protect Him, and eventually release Him to fulfill what, from all eternity, He had been destined to do. But how? They were not wealthy or powerful or even intellectually superior. They had nothing, nothing but faith in God—and a willingness to take a chance for Him.

And because of their "yes," the Savior came.

Mary and Joseph were remarkable people. But they were not unique. Throughout the centuries, and today, people are being asked the same spiritual questions: Do you believe, even when all odds seem stacked against you? Are you willing to live your life His way, rather than your own? Are you courageous enough to ask Him each day, whether in good times or difficult ones: "What would you have me do? Speak, Lord, Your servant is listening."

Everyone faces crossroads; they are part of life. We are all, at some times, frightened, bewildered, angry, hurt, distrustful. And yet it is not the crossroads themselves, but the decisions we make about how to handle them, that truly matter. The people in this book all confronted dilemmas, both large and small. Initially, all were perplexed. But they decided to view these situations through that "second pair of eyes"—eyes that see the spiritual dimension as well as the temporal. Ultimately, they risked an action because they believed it was what God wanted, even though they didn't fully understand His heavenly plan. And they were amazed at the outcomes, the eventual blessings that flowed like rivers from their choices.

Not all of the following episodes happened at Christmas. But each embraces the Christmas message, the same "I will!" that a young couple vowed so very long ago. That's how Mary and Joseph changed the world. That's how we can too.

Upon a Midnight Clear

*And so, as Tiny Tim observed, God
bless us, every one!*

—CHARLES DICKENS
A Christmas Carol

T WAS GOING TO BE A LEAN CHRISTMAS, Barbara and Ray Thill
realized as they surveyed their budget early one December several
years ago. Unexpected medical bills, major repairs on their house in
Berwyn, Illinois, and the ongoing needs of a family of nine young
children had left nothing extra for gifts under the tree.

There were other alternatives, of course. They could take out a loan, or run
up their charge accounts. But the thought was unpalatable; they tried to be good
stewards, and they were certain that unnecessary debt was not in God's plan for
them.

Ray could look for a part-time job at night. "But I felt that the kids and I
needed Ray's presence and help each evening more than the material things his
extra paycheck could provide," Barbara recalls.

Both also knew that if they mentioned their financial difficulties to friends or
family, someone would find a way to help. However, Barbara and Ray were used
to giving help, not getting it, and so they discounted this idea too. They would

say nothing to anyone, and care for their family as best they could. Since all the children needed pajamas, they would buy those, maybe one or two little games to share, and some candy. Hopefully, the kids would understand.

The next day Advent began, and Barbara explained the situation. "Just remember," she told the children gently, "we have a lot more than Baby Jesus did. We have a warm house, good food, enough clothes, and lots of friends. The Holy Family had none of those things in Bethlehem. So this Christmas, just to show Jesus how grateful we are, let's give instead of receive." Her brother, the father of four youngsters, had been out of work for many weeks, and it would be a rough holiday for his family too. "Why don't you each choose one of your toys and wrap it up for Uncle Dick's children," Barbara suggested. "Otherwise, they won't have any celebration at all. And remember 'bread upon the waters.' What we give now, we'll receive a hundredfold in heaven."

The children were quiet for a moment. "That's okay, Mom," one of the boys finally spoke up. "Christmas is about Jesus's birthday anyway." The others nodded, trying to look convinced.

Even the oldest, eleven-year-old Ray Jr.—who had longed for a big red sled for the past three Christmases—hid his disappointment. "I'll buy some stuff for our cousins from my paper route money," he told his mother.

She hugged each child, her beloved ones, her treasures. What is worse than wanting to make people you love happy and not being able to do it? Her heart ached. Should she pray for extra money? No. It would not be inappropriate to do so, she believed, but she knew God had not forgotten them. And if He didn't want her and Ray to provide toys, He would have a good reason. Faith was a decision. And they had decided to leave Christmas in His hands.

Advent continued. The older children attended mass almost every morning on their way to school, and helped the younger ones wrap a few secondhand toys for Uncle Dick's family. At night, around the dinner table, they told one another about the good things in their lives. "Blessings are presents too," Barbara reminded them. "God doesn't wrap them in holiday paper, but they come from Him just the same."

Christmas Eve finally arrived, and it was almost ten P.M. before all the children were asleep. Barbara and Ray laid nine pajama—filled packages under the tree, stuffed nine stockings with candy, and smiled at each other. Their family was together, safe and well, and there was even a little pile of gifts for Uncle Dick's children when the family came over to share a big roasted turkey—and Baby Jesus's birthday cake—tomorrow. Despite their hardships, joy was in the air. Christmas was almost here!

Down the street from the Thills lived Tom and Pat Daly and their family. Tom was not well acquainted with the Thills. He knew the family was large, but would have been hard-pressed to identify anyone in it. Yet during Advent, when his wife heard a rumor that the Thills were going through a hard time, Tom began thinking about them.

What kind of a holiday would they have? Should he inquire? Would it embarrass them? After all, he was virtually a stranger, and they hadn't asked for help from neighbors who knew them far better than he did. What business was it of his, anyway?

Tom tried to put the matter out of his mind. But it continued to nag at him. On December 23 he remembered something. "Say," he asked a teenage boy who had been working for him, "didn't you tell me awhile back that your dad was a toy salesman?"

"He's a jobber," the boy answered. "He calls on stores, shows them toy samples, and takes orders."

"What does he do with those samples when Christmas is over?" Tom was getting an idea.

The boy shrugged. "I dunno. But here's his phone number if you want to find out."

What would he say? Tom wasn't even sure what he wanted to ask. But on the morning of Christmas Eve, he contacted the jobber, who told him to stop by his warehouse. "When I got there, he took me to a room where there were several large toys, some in beat-up cartons," Tom says. "He waved his arm and told me to take whatever I needed."

Tom could hardly believe it. Whatever he needed! But what did he need? He didn't know how many Thill children there were, or their ages or genders. And since his car was quite small, space was going to be limited. What if he chose the wrong things?

Then Tom felt himself relaxing. This whole situation hadn't come about by accident; he was sure of it now. And the same One who arranged it would surely guide him in his selection. Tom looked at the toys. If he was a kid, which ones would *he* like? He took out one of the green plastic bags he'd brought along, and got started.

Barbara and Ray were just getting ready to go to bed when the phone rang. Who could be calling this late on Christmas Eve? Ray answered, spoke briefly, and hung up with a puzzled look. "It was Tom Daly—he lives down the street," he told Barbara.

"Yes, I've met his wife."

"Tom said that he just dropped off a few green bags out in front, some beat-up toy samples for the kids, if we can use them."

If they could use them! Barbara looked outside. There were the bags, lined up on the steps. Ray carried them in. And as she opened them, Barbara's eyes filled with tears.

The toys were beautiful, exquisite, much nicer than anything they'd have been able to afford, even in a prosperous year. Even more astounding, there was one perfectly suited toy for each of the children. There were three dolls for the three girls, a baby toy for the baby, a fire engine almost as large as Larry, and— Barbara blinked in amazement—a large red sled, just what Ray Jr. had always wanted. Thirteen toys in all. Nine for her brood and, incredibly, four extras for her brother's four children. No one had known about their need, or her brother's. Yet Someone had gone shopping just for them.

The next morning the children raced downstairs, and they shouted in wonder at the bounty in the living room. "Mom! You were only kidding about us not getting presents!" six-year-old Eddie shouted in delight.

"No, I wasn't..." Barbara tried to explain.

But Ray Jr. had the best answer. "It's 'bread upon the waters,'" he remarked thoughtfully. "We gave to God, and He gave it back, a hundredfold."

Years later, the Thill family still wonders about the event. There were more lean Christmases, of course, and additional family trials. But the joy of that morning sustained them through much, and is still a cherished memory today. Perhaps the Christmas blessing was not really the unexpected toys, they suggest, but the continued reassurance that God is always with us. No matter how difficult life becomes, we have only to believe—and He will do the rest.[1]

With Songs of Rejoicing

 HE SHOULD NEVER HAVE WAITED so long to tackle the Christmas shopping, Kimberley Little reminded herself as she shifted her bundles from one aching arm to the other. She hated shopping, hated having to brave the crowds and sift through endless piles of merchandise. But there was only so much holiday gift-buying one could do through catalogs, and, of course, the children needed their annual photo taken with Santa Claus. So here she was, imprisoned in a slow-moving "Visit Santa" line, wondering if she might spend the entire holiday season in this Albuquerque mall.

She had to admit she was never "up" at this time of year, no matter how smoothly things went. Her father had died tragically in a plane crash just a few days before Christmas when Kimberley was fourteen, and although many years had passed, she never faced December without feeling echoes of that shock, sorrow, and loneliness. As her faith matured, Kimberley had gotten involved in her church, singing in the choir and teaching her young sons to pray. She didn't doubt that her father was in heaven with Jesus, or that she would see him again. But every year, as Christmas approached, the same nagging question emerged:

"This is all supposed to be so wonderful. So why isn't it?"

Kimberley shifted her packages again, and looked at her three young sons. Their moods seemed no cheerier than hers. One was demanding a ride on the train farther down the mall. Another was hungry. "I hate Christmas!" muttered the eldest, his lip thrust out in frustration.

Kimberley felt guilty. "Moms have so much influence on the spirit of the family," she says. "If we're just a little bit cranky, everyone picks up on it." She didn't want to spoil this season for the children. They shouldn't carry the same vague sadness that she did.

And yet... She glanced around at the other families in line. They were all like hers, she realized: the kids irritable, tired, fighting with one another, the parents grimly Determined to Endure.

Why are we like this? Kimberley wondered. Where was the real Christmas, the spirit of love and peace, the joyful awareness that a Savior had come into the world? How did one cut through the confusion, the fatigue, the pressure—yes, even the sorrowful memories—to find it?

Suddenly, God nudged her. "It couldn't have been anything else," Kimberley says, "because all at once I felt a little tingle, as if something new was happening. And I realized that if I wanted to feel better about myself, I had to take the first step. I had to be brave." But how?

Sing a carol.... The suggestion was already in her heart. She had recently performed a solo in church. She knew how to sing.

But this noisy shopping center was not church. "Oh, no, God, not me," she told Him silently. "You remember how shy I am. People will stare."

Bring Christmas to the mall. Sing.

Kimberley sighed. It was no use. She knew that Voice. And hadn't she asked Him where Christmas was?

Softly she began to sing. "Silent night, holy night..." The couple in front of her, who had been filling out a photography order form, paused and turned around.

"All is calm, all is bright…" Kimberley reached for her youngest son and picked him up. What if they threw her out of the mall, for disturbing the peace?

You're bringing the peace, the answer came. *Sing.*

The children behind her had stopped arguing. "Listen," one whispered to the other. "That lady's singing."

The tips of Kimberley's ears turned red. "Round yon virgin, mother and child…" she went on. Her sons would never speak to her again.

But… Was it her imagination, or did she hear another voice? And another? Yes, the couple in front of her were singing, their order form forgotten. Now the children behind her, and their parents, and the family next to them. Dazed, Kimberley realized that the entire section of the Santa Claus line had joined her. Even her own offspring.

It was true! Little risks could lead to wonderful things. And she *was* feeling better, her spirit soothed, her mind quieted. Maybe Christmas—and its eternal message—was simply as close as anyone allowed it to be.

Voices faded as the song ended. "Let's do 'Angels We Have Heard on High,'" Kimberley suggested to the people around her. It was her eldest's favorite carol, and her dad had always liked it too.

It was going to be a wonderful Christmas.[2]

Any Caring Person

Hate can make a lot of noise. Love and
courage are usually quieter. But in the
end, they're the strongest.
—JANICE COHN
The Christmas Menorahs

URING THE WEE HOURS of Sunday morning, December 8, 1996, after the second night of Hanukkah, someone took a baseball bat and broke the front window of a house in Newtown, Pennsylvania. It might have been considered simple vandalism by the local police except for one significant factor: This house was the only one on the street with a lighted menorah in the window. The perpetrator had deliberately reached through the shattered window, taken the menorah, and smashed it on the ground, breaking all nine bulbs.

The menorah is a symbol of the eight-day Jewish Festival of Lights, also known as Hanukkah, which occurs around the same time of year as Christmas. As a Nativity scene reminds Christians of their heritage and faith, a menorah does so for Jews. It is the symbol of a miracle.

The woman who lives in the house in Newtown did not think of miracles when she found the shattered mess in her front yard. It was not the first time she and her family had been targeted. As a child, she had come with her mother (a Holocaust survivor) and father to the United States to escape persecution in the former Soviet Union. But now, as she viewed the smashed candelabrum, the familiar fear returned.

Lisa Keeling, a young mother, lives down the street, and she heard about the incident when she and her family returned from mass. "A neighbor left a message on my answering machine," Lisa says. "Because I am a former military police officer, he thought I might know the home phone number of our police chief so he could speak to him about the incident right away."

Lisa was appalled. Newtown has about fifteen hundred families, with many cultures and religions represented. Although there was occasional crime, she had never heard of anyone being singled out because of their faith or ethnicity. What effect would this have on the other Jewish families in the neighborhood? she wondered. Would they be intimidated into turning their menorahs off? How would she feel if someone desecrated a statue of Baby Jesus on her lawn? Unless *everyone* was free to follow religious beliefs, no one was.

Lisa was getting an idea. "I'd like to buy a menorah and put it in our front window, so that family will know they're not going through this alone," she told her husband. "If the vandals come back, they'll have us to target too. What do you think?"

Lisa's husband didn't hesitate. "Go for it," he said.

Lisa returned her neighbor's call, and told him about her idea. "Why don't you contact Margie Alexander?" he suggested. "She's doing the same thing."

Margie lived around the corner, and was involved in the Neighborhood Watch program. She had been as horrified as Lisa when she heard the news.

"I work with women in health situations, so I know what pain can look like," Margie says. "When I went to see the woman whose menorah had been smashed, I saw that same pain on her face. I can't do much about the suffering I see at work, but I thought I could do something here." Margie was now driving from store to store looking for menorahs. "But they're almost impossible to find by now," she told Lisa over her car phone.

Lisa began calling stores from home, then relaying locations where the candelabra were available, to Margie. "Buy as many as you can," she suggested, since several Christian neighbors had dropped by to ask for instructions on where to purchase, and how to display, a menorah. Word was getting around.

Sundown—the time for lighting—had almost arrived by the time Margie sped home and distributed all that she had located. "I took down the Christmas lights in one of my windows and put the menorah there, all by itself," Lisa recalls. "I didn't want there to be any doubt about the statement we were making." Was she prepared for trouble? "Maybe," she says. "It passes through your mind. But standing up for a principle is just something you do."

That night when the Jewish victim turned onto her street, she stopped in amazement. Greeting her was a sea of orange lights, shining in silent solidarity from the windows of all eighteen Christian households on her block. We are with you, the warm glow seemed to say. Blinking back tears, she went home, replaced the broken bulbs in her own menorah, and put it back up in her window.

The vandals did not damage any property that night. Eventually police arrested three teenage boys, who admitted that the neighborhood's unexpected show of strength and unity had deterred them from striking again. But they were not the only people affected. As the days of Hanukkah went on, Christian families from nearby blocks began to display menorahs alongside their wreaths and Nativity scenes. "I'd drive past and see a menorah in someone's window and think: 'Wait—I see that family at church—they're not Jewish.' Then it would dawn on me that they were supporting us as we supported the people on my block," Lisa recalls. Other Jewish families in the neighborhood, their confidence rising, turned their menorahs back on too. Word spread, as newspaper reporters and radio talk shows—even one in Israel—contacted the women for interviews. Pastors of local churches discussed the community response in their homilies, and a synagogue invited Lisa and Margie to a service so the congregation could thank them personally. "The rabbi gave us a book about something similar which had happened in Billings, Montana, in 1993," Lisa says. "Because of hate crimes there, the newspaper had printed the picture of a menorah on its front page, and thousands of people had hung the image in their windows. We had never heard about it, yet we ended up doing almost the same thing."[3]

Margie and Lisa are still amazed at all the attention they received because of what to them seems "something any caring person would do." But they're also planning to display menorahs this year. "It's become the most cherished part of my Christmas," Margie says, "because it represents a wonderful lesson I've learned: Just one little step in the right direction can have a domino effect. It can make life better for everyone."

Oh, Holy Night

HE FIRE CALL CAME IN on April 3, 1995 at about one A.M. A blaze
in a two-story apartment building in Rockford, Illinois. Fairly
routine, thought firefighter Paul Grams. He and his partners, Ron
and John, were the first to arrive on the scene.

The first floor was unoccupied, the firefighters learned from neighbors gathering
to watch the drama. But then a bystander ran up. "There's people living upstairs—at
least I think there are!" he shouted. "A lady and her little grandchild."

Possible victims! The scenario shifted as the three men raced into the
building. "The smoke was so thick that it blocked any light, and even muffled
sound," Paul relates. "We searched the apartment but we couldn't find anyone."
The atmosphere seemed strange, even surreal, as they crawled around in
darkness. Paul bumped into someone. "John, is that you?" he asked.

But there was no answer. "Ron?" Paul questioned. Again, no response. But the
presence had been moving, not lying still, like someone overcome by smoke.
Who was it?

Again Paul crawled along, feeling his way. Long minutes passed. Once more, he bumped into something right in front of him. Had other firefighters come into the apartment without the three men knowing it? "Who is this?" Paul demanded.

You will never get out of here alive. The menacing message emanated from whatever was in front of him. It was not in audible words, but somehow it permeated his spirit, bringing fear and peril into the murkiness. "John!" Paul called again. "Is that you?"

No one answered. Paul felt terribly alone. Something was wrong. They had been in the smoke-filled building for almost fifteen minutes, and their air supply would soon be exhausted. But where was the exit? A chill went through Paul, as awareness dawned. The smoke was even denser than before, and nothing could be seen in this endless gray blanket. He and his companions were lost.

You'll never get out of here alive. Again the threatening words came. Paul's skin prickled. Although he couldn't see the voice, he recognized it now. It was Evil.

Sherry Zahorik, of nearby MacChesney Park, Illinois, was having a dream. She was in a room. A foggy room. There were three people crawling in front of her, frantically searching for something. Sherry felt as though she were in their midst, watching them go through this terrible assignment. She could feel their confusion, and something more as well. "There was a terrible demonic presence permeating the room," she says. "Whenever one of these people would bump into something and call the name of his friend, this presence would laugh. And it would say, 'You will never get out of here alive.'"

Abruptly Sherry awakened. She sat up and peered at her alarm clock. Just a little past one A.M. Her chest felt heavy, as if a burden were lying on it, and she could hardly breathe. And... Sherry blinked. She was definitely awake. Yet it seemed as though she was still in the dream too. "I knew in an instant that I should start praying," she says.

Every now and then, Sherry is awakened by an urge to intercede for someone. On the face of it, the impulse seems a bit strange. She never knows exactly what the situation is about or who it is that she's praying for. And why, she has often wondered, should *she* be tapped for this job? Surely her prayers are no more powerful than anyone else's.

However, Sherry wants to be obedient to God whenever He calls on her. And so, despite her questions and her fatigue, she prays.

Tonight, however, the circumstances were different. As Sherry began to pray, she continued to be aware of her dream, and the scenario it had presented. Perhaps this time God was showing her something *specific* so her prayers could be more focused. "Oh God," Sherry began. "You know who and where these people are. Save them, Lord. Remove them from this danger...."

It seemed as if he had been crawling in this blackness forever, Paul thought. Where were the others? Although he couldn't see anything, Paul heard Ron calling the chief on his radio. "Ladder Company No. 1 is lost on the second floor! Someone needs to ventilate the building immediately, so we can find our way out."

"Ron!" Paul called. "Where are you?"

"Over here!" Ron sounded far away. But as Paul attempted to crawl toward him, he bumped into the presence again. It was laughing, a sneering depraved sound. *You will never get out of here alive,* it said.

Where was the chief's answering radio transmission? Where was the sound of glass breaking, as other firefighters smashed windows to remove some of the smoke? Paul strained to hear, but there was no sound at all. An image came to him, from photos that had accompanied a recent article in a firefighter magazine. "It was about a firefighter who had gotten lost in a smoky room, and died when he ran out of air," Paul says. "The pictures showed handprints in the soot on the wall, where he had searched in vain for the window—which was just inches away." Would their deaths be written about in a magazine too?

Paul heard a faint warning bell. It sounded like John's air tank, out of air. Was John already lying unconscious on the floor? Obviously the chief hadn't received Ron's message. Paul grabbed his own radio. "Chief where are you? We're trapped on the second floor, we're lost in the smoke and almost out of air. Break out the windows!" But no answer came. Except the now-familiar whisper of the gloating presence in the room. *You'll never get out,* it said. *Never, never...*

An hour had passed. Assuming that her prayer time wouldn't last too long, Sherry had begun while lying in bed. But each time she tried to finish and fall asleep, she'd felt the same weight on her chest, so heavy that she could neither sleep nor even easily breathe. So she was now in the living room.

Her husband had come out to check on her. "Are you all right?" he'd asked. He was used to her night vigils, and was himself an intercessor, but this situation was lasting an unusually long time.

Oh, how she wanted the comfort of her bed, and sleep. But God had not released Sherry yet. He was telling her something, she knew. The Lord of the Universe, the All-Powerful One, still requested her effort, her love and sacrifice poured out for others in His family, even though she didn't know who they were. Standing in the gap for someone who needed help—that was what being a prayer warrior was all about. One didn't have to understand the "why" of it in order to do it if one was called. Only obedience was required.

Nor did she understand the demonic presence, its role in this terrible event. While praying, she had sensed a vision of a firefighter clawing blindly at a wall, thinking it was a window. These three were in mortal danger, both physically and spiritually, and it would take strong prayers to save them. "I need to keep going," she told her husband. He nodded and went back to bed.

Help would come. It had to. But as he waited for an answer to his radio call, Paul quietly resigned himself to his death, and Ron's and John's too. What a tragedy for the engine company, for all the families and friends involved, especially his youngest daughter, who would turn thirteen tomorrow. But if it was God's will... Paul remembered the voice's sinister whisper: *Never, never...*

Suddenly, as if a cool refreshing wind were blowing through the room, Paul knew that the voice was wrong. Someone somewhere, he realized, was wrestling with this evil presence, doing battle for him and his buddies. Someone was covering him with prayer power, sending reassurance and hope. He *felt* it, in the most tangible way. Peace filled him.

Seconds later John, now completely out of air, found a window and broke it out with both hands. Firefighters on the ground raised a ladder to the window, and John scrambled to safety. Paul and Ron came next, their tanks barely functioning. On the ground, the men filled their lungs with clean pure air, and related what had happened, and the mix-up over the messages. No tenants had been home on the second floor, they were told, nor had other firefighters come to the apartment.

Relieved, the men went back to their work. Later, however, as Paul stood in three-feet-deep water in the basement, he felt again a sense of danger. Looking up, he saw the charred joists, the huge sections of floor burned completely through, and realized that everything could collapse at any moment, trapping him yet again. He had faced enough hazards for one night, he thought, as he clambered up the basement stairs. Whoever was praying for him must still be on duty. He glanced at his watch. Almost five A.M. He should call his wife, Val, before she left for her secretarial job at Rockford's Christian Life Center school, and tell her not to worry if she heard about the fire on the morning news.

Sherry was exhausted. Long ago, she had run out of words, and she was now praying in tongues, a wordless plea arising from somewhere deep in her soul. The evil presence was still there, she knew. And although she no longer envisioned the firefighters crawling in smoke, she knew they were still depending on her. She wouldn't weaken, she told herself. She would go on, as long as necessary, because God had asked her to.

Then, unexpectedly, Sherry felt a lift within her spirit. "It was like something being released," she says. "The situation was over, everything was all right, and I was no longer needed." She would probably never know what had happened. But perhaps she could catch a brief nap before going to her job at Rockford's Christian Life Center school. She crawled into bed, glancing at her clock. It was just before five.

What a hectic day! School secretary Val Grams hadn't had a chance to tell co-workers about her husband's ordeal at the fire. But between phone calls and office details, she continued to give silent thanks to God for sparing Paul and the others. It had been such a close call.

At one point, Val thought she heard Sherry Zahorik, one of the day care workers, telling the principal about being up half the night praying for some people in a fire. Val knew Sherry only slightly, and Sherry had never met Paul, didn't even know he was a firefighter. What a strange coincidence.

It was not until the school day was over, however, that Val had a chance to go out to the playground and ask Sherry to tell her the story. Only then, through their tears, did both women realize what God had done.

Paul Grams and Sherry Zahorik never determined the reason for the evil presence in the burning building that night. Perhaps the site had been used for witchcraft or occult purposes, and spirits continued to linger. Nor do they understand fully how prayer works, or its power to protect others, or why God chooses to communicate through dreams. The link Paul and Sherry shared on one fateful night remains a mystery now, and may be one forever. But they are grateful. And they believe.

The Light of Love

There is a veil covering the unseen world
which not even the strongest...(can)
tear apart. Only faith, poetry, love,
romance can push aside that curtain and
view the supernatural beauty and glory beyond.

—FRANCIS CHURCH
"Is There a Santa Claus?"
New York Sun
September 21, 1897

T WAS THANKSGIVING WEEKEND, 1983, and Andrew Koval, an avid sportsman, decided to take advantage of the holiday. "I'm going hunting," he called to his wife. "I'll be back at five-thirty." Andrew knew his limits, and nature's too; due to an old baseball injury, one of his knees was good for about two hours' worth of walking before pain set in. In addition, darkness would fall at about five o'clock, and since it was already late in the day, his time was short.

Andrew drove to his favorite hunting spot a few miles from his home in rural Cambridge, Ohio, just down the road from a farm where he bought hay every spring. He parked in a familiar hilly area near a field.

He walked awhile, flushed a few grouse out of their hiding places, but never got close enough to try a shot. And, as he slowly realized, his heart wasn't really in the sport today. "My nephew, John Grimes, had died of cancer the past summer," Andrew explains. "We had been very close, working and golfing and socializing together, but most of all, hunting grouse together." Andrew had grieved deeply for the younger man, and now, in this place where they'd spent so much time together, doubts crowded his mind. Was there really a God? If so, did Andrew believe in Him? Was there a heaven? Was John there? Did life, another kind of life, go on after death? As a self-described "lukewarm Catholic," "I still had that little doubt," he says. How could he know for sure?

Andrew had been lost in thought for some time, but it was getting dark, and his expedition was over for today. He started back to the car. "On the way I flushed a grouse and decided to follow it to get off at least one shot," he recalls. "The bird flew in the opposite direction, but being in familiar territory, I wasn't concerned." As the sun began to set, Andrew lost sight of the bird.

No problem, he told himself The terrain was wooded, but he knew about where he was. If he walked back in a straight line, he ought to reach the car in about fifteen minutes. And that's what he did; at least that's what he thought he did. But soon Andrew realized he had passed the same marker twice. He was going in a circle.

What to do? "I was wearing a light hunting vest, and it was getting colder," he says. "My knee had started to hurt. I kept walking west, trying to reach an area that I recognized." Surely he would hit a road soon, and be able to flag down a vehicle. He walked and walked, only to realize that he was again traveling in a circle. Oh, if only John were here! His resourceful young nephew would surely have found the way out of this maze.

Cold and tired, his knee throbbing, Andrew knew his wife and son were going to be very worried. How long would it be before they alerted the sheriff? Should he try to build a temporary shelter and wait to be found? But people had died that way, freezing to death before help arrived. Could he withstand a winter night with a vest his only warmth?

There was another option, he slowly realized. He could pray. It had been a long time since Andrew had really talked to the Father. But if God was everywhere, even here in this lonely forest, He would surely hear. And if John was with Him... Andrew sat down under a tree. "God," he whispered, "I don't know if You're listening. But if You are, I need help."

Minutes passed. More minutes. Slowly a plan came to him. He should climb the highest hill, look for a light and head straight for it. *Look for the light.* Was God talking to him? Andrew didn't know. But there was a high hill nearby.

Gathering the last of his strength, Andrew scrambled to the top. At last! He ought to be able to see a lot of the countryside from here. But ... He could hardly believe it. There was no light visible, not in any direction. No distant signal blinking from a house or store, not even car headlights moving in the blackness.

It hadn't been a heavenly message, after all. Yet the feeling of comfort, of guidance, had been so real. *Look for the light.* The real light in his life ought to be God, he realized, no matter what happened to him now, or in the future. And it would be. His leg ached and his fear of freezing was strong. But he had felt the light, just a little, and he wouldn't let it dim again.

Slowly, he turned away. He would go back down the hill and...wait. Andrew gazed into the blackness once more, his eyes narrowing. Was it a mirage? No, there in the distance...It was a light! Not in the same direction as his car should be, but Andrew had run out of choices. He would go toward it. Whoever owned it would have a phone, or warmth, or some way to help him.

"I must have walked at least another mile, but I was able to keep the light in view the whole time, despite the trees," Andrew says. Unexpectedly, he came upon the road where he had parked his car. And there it was!

Astonished, Andrew scrambled inside and turned on the engine and the heater full blast. Soon he was blissfully warm and content, as if this terrible experience had never happened. He should get home now, to relieve his wife's fears.

But oddly, he could still see the light, streaming from a field about three or four hundred yards down the road, near the farm he visited each spring. He was so late already—it wouldn't make much difference if he drove down and looked to see exactly what had brought him safely out of his ordeal. He did.

"There in the field was a two-story house, with every room brightly lit, and two flood-lights on each corner," he says. "There were people working all around, both inside and out." Andrew knew this piece of land, he realized—it was owned by a realtor and was for sale in five-acre lots. He had no idea that a house had already been built here. "I thought it was strange that I hadn't known, and also that every room was blazing with light and there was so much activity," he says. But he had his answer, and he turned around in the house's driveway and went home.

It was almost nine o'clock by the time Andrew arrived, and his worried wife and son were preparing to call the sheriff and arrange a search party. But he assured them that he was none the worse for wear, and told them about the house. Andrew's wife hadn't heard about the newly built house either. But hadn't it been fortunate that he had seen it!

Andrew didn't grouse-hunt for the rest of the season. But the following spring, he decided it was time to visit the local farmer and buy his hay. As Andrew turned onto the same country road where he had seen the house, he looked for it. Now he would see if it was as big and beautiful—and busy—during the day as it had looked on that memorable night. Maybe he would even pull into the driveway, ring the bell, and tell the owner how his marvelous lights had probably saved Andrew's life.

Andrew approached the lot where the house had been. But there was no building there, or anywhere around it. The area looked just as it had last spring when Andrew had come to buy his hay. Completely deserted.

Odd…He was certainly looking at the same spot where he had been that night—he remembered the familiar markers, the hills beyond, the place where the driveway had been. Had the people who built the house belatedly discovered that their well was inadequate? This had happened before, Andrew knew, and when it did, an owner would occasionally move his house to another lot.

Andrew passed the lot, and pulled into the farm driveway. The farmer's sister came out to greet him. After purchasing his hay, Andrew paused for a moment. "I was wondering what happened to that big new house down the road," he asked.

The woman looked puzzled. "What house?" she asked.

"The one with all the lights. In the new subdivision. Did they have to move it because of a bad well?"

"I don't know what you're talking about. The builder never sold any of those lots. There has never been a house there."

"But…" Andrew felt a shiver. The woman was looking at him as if he were odd. But he knew what he had seen.

Andrew has never found any evidence that a house was on that lot, nor anyone else who ever saw it. But he is as sure today as he was that night that it was there. "I have come to believe that God was responsible for it," he says, "because the whole experience completely resolved any doubts I may have had about Him, and about the continuance of life after death on earth." And perhaps his nephew was involved too. One never knows, when one is willing to ask, just what marvels the Light will bring.

Angels We Have Heard
(and Seen) on High

The footprints of an angel are love. And where
there is love, miraculous things can happen.
—ANGELS IN THE OUTFIELD

WELVE-YEAR-OLD NANCY PETTI (now Doran) and her family had recently come to the Bronx, in New York City, from their native Italy. It had been a decision born out of great hope, for many times Nancy's father had attempted to start his own business in Italy, and at one point had even left the family temporarily to try the same thing in Germany. Eventually Nancy's parents had decided that America offered the best chance of professional success, for themselves and their children.

Nancy, her older brother, and her younger sisters had been excited about the move, but apprehensive too. What did America look like? Was it similar to the movies they saw? Would they make new friends? Of course there would be challenges as they became accustomed to an unfamiliar language, and new housing, jobs, and schools. But God had guided them through this formidable journey, and Nancy's parents firmly believed He would continue to take care of them.

Nancy wished she had the same faith as her mother and father. Yes, she was becoming accustomed to much in her new land. But no one had warned her about the cold weather. As that first winter tightened its grip on New York, Nancy could hardly believe how brutal the cold was, especially inside their apartment. "We didn't have much money, so this top-floor apartment was all we could afford," she remembers. "But the landlord refused to provide steam heat, and the temperature was so low you could see your breath. We usually wore coats and blankets during the day, and the oven was always on, with a pot of water boiling on the stove top for steam."

Even worse were the nights. Without a thick layer of blankets, "it felt as though the apartment had no walls and we were actually sleeping outside," Nancy says.

Oh, why had they risked everything to come here? Nancy felt abandoned and lost. Soon it would be Christmas, a time to rejoice and give thanks. But it was hard to be grateful when your fingers and toes ached, and you couldn't do your homework or even sleep because you shivered so much.

One bitter night, Nancy awoke and lay in the dark. She had curled into a little ball, trying to keep as warm as possible, but it wasn't working. She felt numb, as if she had turned to ice, and her thin blanket had slipped off her shoulders. Nancy tried to pull the blanket up to her chin. But her arms were stiff; they wouldn't work! Was she freezing to death? "Oh, God, I'm so cold I can't even pull up my covers," she prayed. "Please help me."

Suddenly the room began to glow. Brighter and brighter... What was happening? Nancy rubbed her eyes in wonder. There, right in front of her, stood a beautiful angel. Italy was filled with statues of angels—Nancy knew what these beings were. But this angel wasn't made of plaster. She was alive! "She had shimmering blonde hair, her eyes were a brilliant blue, and she wore a flowing white gown," Nancy remembers. "Even more extraordinary was the light that radiated from within and all around her." What a beautiful creature! And she was visiting *Nancy,* in this cold, drab apartment! Nancy drank in the sight.

Tenderly, the angel smiled at her. Then she bent over, gently lifted Nancy's blanket, and pulled it up to the girl's chin. Nancy felt a burst of warmth, safety, and love. Instantly the freezing room seemed filled with sunshine. Then the angel vanished.

It was a happier Christmas that year than Nancy had expected. She didn't know it yet, but the risk her family took in coming to this new land would soon be rewarded: her father would open a successful Italian restaurant, Full Moon, which still operates in the Bronx today. Nor did she know that, in future winters, she would never again be bothered by the cold.

But she did know one thing for certain: God was closer than she had ever imagined, and all she needed to do was simply reach out to Him. His angels could find her wherever she was.

Elouise Carey had always been a nervous driver, especially on expressways. Once while traveling the busy I-95 near Swarthmore, Pennsylvania, she had heard a clinking noise in the front of her car. "I couldn't stop anywhere, so I just went on to my friend's house, and told her husband about the noise," Elouise recalls. "He checked it for me."

A few minutes later, her friend's husband reentered the house, looking pale. All the lug nuts on the right front wheel—the pieces that keep the wheel on the car—had fallen off, and were lying inside the hubcap. "I don't know what was holding this wheel on," he explained, "but I think you were very lucky, Elouise."

Luck? Perhaps. But Elouise believed in angels more than luck. She liked to think that God sent them to watch over her whenever she drove.

As Christmas approached that year, however, and Elouise spent more and more hours in her car, her apprehension about driving anywhere increased. One day in mid-December, thinking about the expressway traffic, she almost called off a shopping trip with a friend. But before picking up the phone, Elouise thought about it. Wasn't fear contrary to the whole message of Christmas, and Christianity? If she truly believed in everything she thought she did, then there had to be a better way to deal with her problem. There was. Elouise decided to pray, and go.

"Again we took I-95 to the mall," she relates. "We shopped, had lunch, shopped some more, and drove home about fifty-five miles per hour at the busiest time of day, with cars speeding all around us." Elouise dropped her friend off, drove to her own house, pulled into the driveway, turned off the engine...

...And the steering wheel dropped right into her lap. Horrified, Elouise looked at it, remembering the episode with the lug nuts. Not again! How had she and her friend survived? If her steering wheel had fallen off on the expressway, they most certainly would have been killed.

But they hadn't been killed. And suddenly a feeling of peace stole over her, as she remembered a night many centuries before when an angel had brought the same message: "Fear not." Jesus and His angels were indeed watching over her today, just as they always did, and had sent her an early Christmas gift to tell her so.

The cold rain had gone on since morning, keeping Bob Nance from his construction job, and increasing his worry over finances. A lost day's pay was hard to make up. His family was getting low on groceries, and with Christmas coming... He paced back and forth in his little house, as his wife and mother-in-law fixed dinner in the kitchen and his three children played nearby. What if this deluge continued through tomorrow?

"Dinner's ready!" Bob's wife called. Everyone headed for the table. Just then, Bob heard a knock on the front door. Who could be out in this storm?

He opened it just a crack, to keep the cold air from coming in. On the porch stood a man about fifty years old, wearing a black suit, top coat, and hat. Water ran down from the hat's brim and dropped onto the man's already saturated coat. His shoes were sodden. "How can I help you?" Bob asked.

Despite his rumpled appearance, the stranger smiled. "The Lord said I should stop and talk with you," he said.

Bob frowned. Was the man a crackpot? Surely he shouldn't invite him inside. And yet, there was something about him.... Bob remembered the innkeeper in Bethlehem so many centuries ago. He had always wondered whether he could have found room for the Holy Family if the inn had been his. Well, he didn't have a hotel, but he did have a warm home. "Come in out of this weather, sir," he said, throwing open the door. "Let me take your wet things and dry them."

The visitor took off his hat, and Bob's oldest child, Dan, carried it to the kitchen to warm by the stove. Bob reached for the man's coat. "No, I'll just lay it over the back of this chair," the stranger said. The coat began to drip on the wooden floor. It must have been soaked completely through, Bob thought.

The family made room for their unexpected visitor at the dinner table, and shared their modest meal with him. Conversation flowed freely and pleasantly. "We didn't talk of anything specifically religious," Bob recalls, nor did our guest tell us much about himself." Yet the little scene seemed right, somehow, as if everyone there was sharing in an unspoken benediction. Bob felt his worries gently lifted from his shoulders. Things would get better, he knew. Just as the food had stretched tonight to include the stranger, the Lord would stretch Bob's meager resources and help him care for his family.

As the meal ended, the visitor got up. "Thank you all for this wonderful dinner," he smiled. "I'll have to be moving on now."

Young Dan brought back the stranger's hat, still quite wet, and gave it to him. Bob picked up the coat lying over the chair, and held it as the man slipped it on. The two walked to the door together and shook hands, and the visitor departed into the rain. Bob closed the door. And then, the realization hit him.

The stranger's coat had been completely dry.

But it couldn't have dried in that short time—the floor around the chair was still slippery with puddles! Bob flung open the front door. Although he had a clear view of his entire street, and the stranger had had only seconds to walk away, no one was there.

Slowly Bob closed the door. "I think we just fed an angel," he told his wife. And the blessings the angel brought would last, he knew, not just for Christmas, but all year long.

The Visitor

NN McALLISTER CLARK'S FATHER had died recently, and she was still feeling his loss. And something else as well: a curious woundedness that surfaced at unexpected moments. In part, this was because she and her father—while loving and loyal to one another—had never been close, in the way good friends are close. Ann had been a lifelong lover of books, had majored in literature in college, and had recently opened a used book store in her small town of Middleville, Michigan. Mr. McAllister, by contrast, was a lawyer, apparently uninterested in all but the driest of writings.

But Ann's sense of loss had deepened shortly after the funeral, when she had found his college diplomas and realized with shock that he too had majored in literature, at the University of Michigan. Why had he never told her, never alluded to a shared interest that might have helped bridge the gap between them? Ann felt cheated, almost embittered at the missed opportunity.

One day while boxing his law books, she found a fine 1909 set of Harvard

Classics, each volume bearing his signature. "Very lightly, I ran my fingers over the inscriptions," Ann says. "Touching them somehow made me feel his presence." She discovered other excellent works too, a set of the International Library of Famous Literature, Lord Morley's *Works of Voltaire*, and more. But the Harvard Classics were her favorites. Why hadn't he written his name in any of his other books? Ann would never know. But the Classics made him seem closer. She would keep this treasured collection always.

The family finished packing Mr. McAllister's belongings, and everyone took some keepsakes. They held a sale, then arranged an auction for the leftovers. "Not those," Ann cautioned the auctioneer's burly sons, as she pointed to the boxes containing the Classics. "Just take the law books. The rest will go home with me." And that's what she thought had happened. Until three days after the auction, when she discovered that the set of Harvard Classics was not in the boxes she had taken. Every volume, each with her father's signature, was gone.

Ann fought down panic. You're a former antiques dealer, she reminded herself sternly. You know how to trace sales records. You'll find the books.

But it was no use. The Classics had apparently been sold quickly, then again, and yet again. Hopelessly gone. Probably gathering dust on someone's top shelf halfway around the country. To her, the final link with her father—now forever broken.

Swallowing her sorrow, Ann returned to her new project, the used book store. There were few customers, and she worried about whether she could keep going. Yet the store brought her a small measure of comfort, and she needed that right now.

One quiet morning, an elderly man wandered in. He did not seem to be in the market for a used book, Ann thought, noticing the perspiration on his forehead, the eyes slightly glazed. As a diabetic, Ann had occasionally come across fellow sufferers; this man might be one. On the other hand, he might be mentally disturbed. Was she in danger, or was he? "Do you need help?" she asked.

"Why do you ask?" he responded, somewhat belligerently.

Should she call 911, and turn him over to others? No, there was something about him, something vulnerable. Ann knew what that felt like; wasn't she herself in the process of healing? Surely she could reach out, just a little. "What can I do for you?" she asked again, gently, as if approaching a frightened deer.

"I'm George, and I've just gotten out of the hospital," the man explained. "I have high blood sugar—but I knew I was going to be sick before it happened. I see things that others cannot see."

Ann thought again about 911. Her visitor probably did have diabetes, but he was obviously delusional as well. "Do you have anyone at home to care for you?" she asked.

"My wife. But she's tired of all these things." Yesterday on the drive to the hospital, George explained, the road had been strewn with beautiful flowers. Like a sign that all would be well. But his wife couldn't see them. On another occasion, his deceased mother had appeared at the foot of his bed, holding a small lyre. She had handed it to George to play, and he had done so, although he had never played any musical instrument before. His wife had slept right through it. There were other examples too, lots of them. . . .

Ann wondered if George was running a high fever. People hallucinated during fevers, didn't they? "George"—she put a kindly hand on his arm—"you've just gotten out of the hospital and your blood sugar is out of whack."

"So?"

"So I care about you. Why don't you go home, have a light supper, take a warm bath, get into bed, and listen to some soothing music. Rest and sleep. Your body needs it."

"You don't believe me," George said. Then he smiled, and went out the front door. Ann smiled back. He had not taken offense, and that was good. But would he get home safely?

Ann worried about George all evening. Perhaps she should search for him, or tell someone about him. But that might cause more problems for him, instead of soothing the ones he already had. Maybe she shouldn't have gotten involved. Yet, wasn't that what life was supposed to be about, watching out for one another? Finally, she decided: If she didn't see George the following day, she would take action.

Shortly after she opened the store the next morning, however, George arrived. A rejuvenated George, with pink healthy skin and smiling eyes. "George!" Ann exclaimed. "You look great!"

He had been touched by her concern, he explained, and he had gone home and done everything she suggested. "I don't think I have slept that well in months. And it was all because of you."

She hadn't done much, she tried to explain. Just what any fellow diabetic would do.

But George had more to say. "I came in here yesterday because I knew you were lonely and worried about business picking up." How had he known? Ann wondered. Was it so obvious after all? "I wanted to help you," George was explaining, "and you ended up helping me instead. So I've brought you a present. Some books."

Just what Ann needed. More used books that no one would probably ever buy. She tried to look enthusiastic and grateful as George went out to his car, and carried in two brown paper bags. It was enough that he seemed more normal today. She could always get rid of this latest batch after he left.

Only… When she pulled out the first few, she realized that they were Harvard Classics. "George! I lost a set of my father's just like these!" George nodded, as if he knew all about it. Ann continued to unpack the books. Amazing. These covers were the same as the lost set, reddish maroon leather.

Slowly she opened the first book. There was her father's signature.

It was impossible. Yet the set was complete, each volume bearing the familiar inscription. Her father's final gift, returned as a result of her own compassion. She touched the writing, then lifted tear-filled eyes to George. "How...

But the question was too big, and George would only smile. "You see?" he told her. "I do know things."

George visited the store several times after delivering the treasured books. "I believe he was lonely, and needed company," Ann says. "I just let him talk." He never explained how he had gotten the books, and she never asked. Later she sold the store to an employee. Now, along with pursuing a writing career, she runs a rare books business on the Internet.

But whenever Ann becomes discouraged or lonely, she remembers the blessing of that moment of discovery, her father's unexpected message of love and connection, the awareness that what goes around truly comes around. And she touches the signature again.

All Ye Faithful

Many smalls make a great.
—AFRICAN PROVERB

AZEL WHITNEY, OF WOODLAND HILLS, CALIFORNIA, was concerned when her grown daughter, Elizabeth,* announced she was taking a sight-seeing trip, alone, to Yellowstone National Park. Driving through such wilderness would be a bit hazardous for anyone, but Elizabeth had been stricken with multiple sclerosis ten years ago, and had gradually become too disabled to work or even walk. "She lives independently, drives a car with hand-controls, and brings her wheelchair wherever she goes," Zazel explains, "but I still worry about her." Although Elizabeth had camped outdoors many times, on this trip she was planning to stay at a hotel. Despite this added protection, Zazel was still nervous. But she knew she couldn't dissuade her courageous daughter, so she began to pray for Elizabeth instead.

A day or two after Elizabeth had left on the trip, Zazel stopped at a gas station on her way home from work. A woman wearing a nurse's uniform, with a stethoscope sticking out of her pocket, approached Zazel as she filled her car's tank. The woman had apparently been crying.

Zazel looked up. "What's the matter? Are you in trouble?"

---

* Not her real name.

"Yes, I am," the nurse replied tearfully. "I had a flat tire on the freeway, and had no spare. A nice man stopped, and drove me here to buy a tire. But my car is old, and this station doesn't sell oversize tires." She wiped her eyes.

"What are you going to do?" Zazel asked.

"The man said he knew where he could pick up a used tire of that size for thirty dollars," the nurse said. "He left, and I went to the ATM station next door to get thirty dollars to repay him when he comes back. But I've lost my wallet, with my card in it, and I have no cash...." Tears filled her eyes again. "Could you... could you *possibly* lend me thirty dollars?"

Zazel thought for a moment. She didn't have any cash either. But she could write a check to this helpful man, and the nurse could reimburse her later. That is, if she believed the nurse's story. Actually, she didn't. The whole situation seemed contrived— why would an anonymous passerby spend time buying a tire for someone he didn't know? And was it logical that this woman would lose her wallet just when she most needed it? Besides, Zazel had been raised to be leery of strangers.

Yet, what if the story was true? What would Jesus do in such a situation? What would He have her do? Zazel often asked herself that question. And when the nurse kept weeping, Zazel decided to help.

The nurse had written the man's name on a piece of paper, so Zazel wrote a check for thirty dollars to him. Then the women exchanged addresses and phone numbers, and sat in Zazel's car, waiting for the man to return with the tire. By now the nurse had calmed down. "You are so sweet to help me," she told Zazel. "What would I have done without you?"

But what would the nurse do if this man never reappeared? Zazel wondered. It was getting late, and Zazel had other chores to complete. Reluctantly, she left the woman at the gas station. "I'll mail you your money as soon as I get home," the nurse called after her. "Thanks again!"

During the next week, Zazel thought often of the nurse, and wondered how things had worked out. She would phone her to find out, as soon as she received the money. But a week passed, then another, and no payment arrived. Zazel felt foolish. Maybe there hadn't been a helpful man and a flat tire after all—maybe she had simply been the victim of a clever scam. Why hadn't she been wise enough to spot it? She still had the nurse's registry phone number, if that wasn't a fake too.

"Should I call her and ask about the money?" Zazel asked her husband.

"Why?" her husband answered. "You did a good thing, and you're only out thirty dollars. Let it go."

He was right, Zazel knew. Only her pride had been injured. Jesus knew her motive, and His view was the one she needed to trust. She tossed the nurse's number away. And when the check came back, endorsed with the name Zazel had inscribed, she filed it away without attempting to trace the man.

Zazel's daughter Elizabeth returned from her trip on a Saturday night, and Zazel met her at church the next morning. "How did everything go?" she asked, relieved to see her daughter in one piece.

"Oh Mom, it was great, but you'll never guess what happened," Elizabeth exclaimed. "I had a flat tire in the wilds of Utah on my way home." Since she couldn't walk, she held up her sun visor that says NEED HELP, CALL POLICE.

"A nice person stopped and changed my tire, so I drove to a roadside park to have my lunch," Elizabeth went on. "Another tourist sat down next to me, and when I told her what happened, she reminded me that my spare was just for short trips—I couldn't get all the way to Los Angeles on it. But what was I supposed to do now? How could I find a tire big enough for my car, especially in such a remote area? Plus I didn't have any cash left, just a credit card."

Zazel was starting to get goosebumps. The story sounded familiar.

"The tourist volunteered to get me a secondhand tire that was the right size,"

Elizabeth went on. "It took a lot of trust for me to wait there in the park, all by myself. What if it got dark and she didn't return?"

"But did she?"

"Yes, with the tire. But when I asked for her address so I could send her the money for it, she said, 'Oh, we're church people—we do things like this for others all the time.' She wouldn't let me reimburse her, Mom. Can you believe it?"

Zazel could. And suddenly, she saw her own situation through *spiritual* eyes. Maybe she had not been the victim of a clever con artist, after all. Perhaps she had been given a chance to sow something another could reap, to send ahead a blessing that her own daughter would soon need. Did such things happen? How would she ever know?

In Bonnie's* case, the outcome was different. "Every morning when I got off the commuter train, I'd pass this homeless man on my way to work," she relates. "I have never gotten involved with people like this because I have mixed feelings— would my donation buy drugs for them, or enable them to stay helpless?" Perhaps. Yet Bonnie seemed drawn to this particular vagrant. Like Zazel, she found herself asking a different question: What would Jesus have her do?

Gradually Bonnie made eye contact with this man. Brief conversations followed. His name was Phil, he told her, and he had been on the streets about a year. Beyond that, he would not elaborate. Sometimes Bonnie's only connection with Phil was a smile and a cheery greeting. At other times, she'd bring him a sandwich, or give him some coins. "The people at my office teased me unmercifully," she says. "They felt I was a 'soft touch,' and hopelessly gullible." But she kept on; somehow it just seemed right.

One day, however, Phil was not at his usual post. Weeks passed, and he didn't

---

* Not her real name.

return. Bonnie was concerned, but the merchants and police officers along her route didn't know what had happened to him. Gradually, she forgot too.

Until one morning when, as she passed the corner, someone called her name. She turned around. Coming toward her was Phil! But not the same disheveled beggar she had befriended over a year ago. No, this Phil was clean—shaven, clear—eyed, wearing a suit and a smile. "Phil!" she gasped. "What happened to you?"

"*You* did, Bonnie." He was standing in front of her now, and she could hardly believe the change in him.

"Me? I didn't..."

"Oh, but you did. You and two men. For that whole year I lived on the streets, you three were the only ones who saw me—as a *person*. You looked at me, and talked to me. One day I asked myself: If there are three people in the world who believe in me, why can't I believe in me? So I went into rehab, and here I am."

He had a new job, he explained, and wouldn't be downtown anymore. So he had come to his old corner one last time, to see if he could locate the three who had changed his life. "I found the men yesterday," Phil explained. "I was just waiting for you."

"Whatever you do to the least of My children, you do to Me...." Bonnie could hardly see Phil through the tears in her eyes. But she knew now the Source of that unusual urge to "get involved," if only in a small way. How glad she was that she had obeyed!

Zazel Whitney didn't get to see the end of her story— and may never know the "why" of it. Bonnie was more fortunate. But often, we aren't meant to control or even understand results. It's enough that He has asked, "Will you do this for Me?" and we have answered, "Yes."4

Hope Is Where the Heart Is

Have you seen God's Christmas tree in the sky,
With its trillions of tapers blazing high?
—ANGELA MORGAN
"Christmas Tree of Angels"

ONNA CLESZYKOWSKI WAS BORN with kidneys that were too small. She didn't know it until she was almost twenty and began having terrible headaches. Tests revealed kidney problems as well as high blood pressure. In 1981, she started dialysis at Sherman Hospital in Crystal Lake, Illinois, beginning with one three-hour session each week. Gradually her needs required her to go twice a week for treatments.

Although dialysis kept her alive and able to work at a bank, it was not the sort of life Donna had envisioned. She was beginning to realize that, because of her shaky health, her dreams of meeting a wonderful man, getting married, and raising a family would probably never come true. And although she tried to be grateful for the blessings she did enjoy, especially her supportive extended family, sometimes life seemed very hard indeed. "The question 'Why me?' came to mind from time to time," she admits.

One of the bright spots in Donna's life was Kathy, another dialysis patient. The women's appointments were usually on the same days, and they formed a friendship. Sick since childhood, Kathy had been on dialysis for six years when Donna met her, and she seemed resigned to it. Donna, however, still hoped for a way out.

The nurses who treated them thought both women should seek kidney transplants. "Have you ever considered it?" Donna asked Kathy one day.

"Yes," Kathy answered slowly. "In fact, my younger brother Ray told me on my wedding day—when he was sixteen—that he'd give me one of his kidneys whenever I was ready."

"That's wonderful! Are you going to do it?" Donna asked.

Kathy shook her head. "Transplants aren't foolproof, Donna. I've known dialysis patients who died after receiving a kidney. And what about Ray? Would it be fair for him to take this kind of risk for me?"

"Maybe he'd *want* to take it, if it meant you'd be well," Donna pointed out. Ray Pokorny sounded like a great brother. But Kathy shook her head. She had thought about it, but she was too afraid to take the chance.

Donna knew there were complications with transplants. At least on dialysis, she was alive. And yet she often wondered, what kind of life was she having? She had always been close to the Lord, and she had asked Him many times for a healing. He had said no—at least she assumed He had—and she could live with that. But *should* she, if there was something she could do to change the situation?

Donna continued her dialysis, but her condition worsened, and eventually she had to quit her job. "During that time, I read a lot of books, and frequently visited my relatives," she recalls. But her life was narrowing, and on Christmas Day, 1984, Donna looked around at her loved ones with a sinking heart. Her health was shakier, and the longer she stayed on dialysis, the worse she was probably going to get. Would she even be here next Christmas? Her uncle Johnny, carrying out a Polish custom of sharing blessed water, had just wished

Donna "health and a transplant." But she hadn't even put herself on the list. Should she try for a miracle?

Yes. Somehow, it seemed right. She had prayed, and she had endured. If God had anything else in mind for her, she was willing to try it.

Donna signed up for a kidney a few weeks after the holidays. "I told Kathy about my decision, and the nurses again tried to encourage her to accept Ray's kidney, but she didn't show much interest," Donna says.

On September 2, 1985, Donna received a cadaver kidney at Rush Presbyterian St. Luke's Hospital in Chicago. The operation was a complete success, and when Kathy came to see her, she could hardly believe her eyes. Donna had weighed 105 pounds at the time of her surgery—and in just a few days, had lost thirty pounds of water. "You're so tiny!" Kathy exclaimed. But Donna was healthy too—everyone could see that. And life began to change for her, almost immediately.

"I had energy, and I couldn't remember ever feeling so well!" Donna explains. "Now I could eat foods that had been all but forbidden before, so I gradually gained weight." She told the bank she'd be able to return to her job after Christmas. And she started another habit as well, reciting each day a petition she had found in a little book. "Prayer for a Good Spouse," it was called. And why not? If the Lord had restored her health, He might have other blessings in mind for her too.

One unexpected benefit from her own surgery was the change in Kathy. Impressed and reassured by Donna's rapid recovery, Kathy finally overcame her longtime fears. "I asked my brother if he remembered volunteering his kidney all those years ago," Kathy said elatedly one day while visiting Donna. "And he said, 'sure—let's go for it!' He's a perfect match, Donna. Isn't that wonderful?" Just a few weeks later, Kathy underwent surgery at the same hospital, with the same positive results. Ray too recovered with no difficulties. What a fine brother

Ray was, Donna thought. To risk something like this, for no other reason than love. She hoped she'd get the chance to meet him someday, and tell him so.

The 1985 Christmas season was far different than the one before. It was Donna's parents' turn to host the extended clan for Christmas Eve, so Donna bought champagne for a celebration toast. "I thought for a long time about what to say, how to express my gratitude for their love and support, and for all the prayers that had been answered," she says. In the end, she simply raised her glass and thanked them all.

By the time Uncle Johnny came to her with the traditional blessing of water, most of the guests were weeping. "Donna," he said simply, "for you I wish continued good health, and whatever you wish for."

Whatever she wished for... Despite the joy of this day Donna still held some fear in her heart. Was she truly cured, or might her kidney problems recur? Would she always be alone, or would there be a special someone in her life one day? Later, when the household quieted, Donna looked out the window into the star-studded Christmas sky. "Jesus," she prayed quietly, "You know my situation. I'm as vulnerable as you once were. And I need a sign. Are things going to be okay for me now?"

Suddenly, a shooting star blazed across the heavens! She had never seen one before, and her eyes filled with tears. It was her Christmas gift, the reassurance she had hoped for. She would continue the way she had begun, including her faithful recitation of the Prayer for a Good Spouse, and wait upon the Lord.

In January, Kathy invited Donna to a family gathering at her mother's house. The two hadn't met since Kathy's surgery, and they wanted to share transplant experiences. Donna found the apartment and rang the bell. No one answered. She rang again. Did she have the wrong address, or the wrong date?

Suddenly, a young man wrenched open the door, his hair still wet from the shower. "Hi!" he grinned. "You're...

"Donna Cleszykowski." She put out a hand. "I'm a friend of Kathy's..."

The young man took her hand, his eyes warm. "I know who you are," he said. "I'm Ray Pokorny."

Donna does not say that it was love at positively first sight, although Ray might disagree. (To this day he remembers exactly what she was wearing that night, even her shoes and purse.) But he proposed just a few months later. And she didn't have to consider very long. "Ray," she asked him one day just before the wedding, "did you ever ask God for anything in return, after you decided to take the risk and be a donor?"

Ray looked somewhat abashed. "I asked God to use my kidney to give Kathy a long healthy life," he answered, "and..."

"And...?"

"That if He gave *me* anything, it would be a girl for me to love and marry."

Donna has long since passed the Prayer for a Good Spouse on to someone else, and she and Ray are enjoying the additional blessing of their adopted son, Stevie. God had not said no to her at all, she has discovered. He had simply said, not yet. There were events that had to happen, love that had to be given before her own answers could come, and the plan sometimes proceeds more slowly than we understand. But it does proceed, for God is never late. The Pokornys can attest to that.[5]

The Power of Prayer

*Seems that God is looking more for ways to get us home
than for ways to keep us out. I challenge you to find one
soul who came to God seeking grace and did not find it.*

—MAX LUCADO
When God Whispers Your Name

IKE AND SUSAN RHEAUME are a well-liked spiritual couple whose
lives revolved around their two sons, Mike Jr. and Andy. Although
Andy was somewhat of a loner, he was also an obedient son and an
affectionate brother. That was why it was such a shock to Mike and
Susan when Andy turned eighteen and abruptly announced he was moving out
of the house. "I just don't want to live here anymore," he told his parents. "I'll
finish high school, but I want to be on my own."

"Why?" Susan asked, stunned.

Andy shrugged. He couldn't offer any answers, at least none that his parents
could comprehend.

During his final semester Andy stayed with friends, or lived on the streets.
He attended classes and wrestling practice every day, and caused no problems.
In the absence of delinquency, drug use, or truancy, school officials told Mike
and Susan that they couldn't intervene. Andy was healthy, and a legal adult.

There was no way his parents could force him to live in their house.

After graduation, Andy seemingly had a change of heart. He moved back home and prepared to attend a Christian college on a wrestling scholarship. But after one semester, he lost interest in school. He returned home briefly, then left again—for a life on the streets.

Mike and Susan were heartbroken. Their son, part of the homeless population! It was hard to bear the thought of him, cold and hungry, choosing to live in a cardboard box or other appalling surroundings. "I would go out looking for him, to try and persuade him to come home, or to bring blankets and food," Mike says. "Sometimes he lived in a rusted-out car near a junkyard—I'd leave things there for him." But despite their efforts, Andy grew more and more distant. Eventually he took a job selling magazine subscriptions, and left the area.

Several months later, Mike and Susan got a call from Andy. He was in South Dakota with his girlfriend, who was expecting a child. Could they come home?

Mike and Susan longed to rescue their son, although they were hesitant about these new circumstances. They drove to South Dakota, collected the couple, and explained on the way back that the young people could live with them until the baby was born, if certain conditions were met. "We wanted Andy to join the mainstream, to get a job and straighten up," Mike says. "We told them we wouldn't give them access to our credit cards, or money to spend. They would have to treat us fairly, and take responsibility for themselves." Andy and his girlfriend initially agreed to the terms.

But shortly before Thanksgiving, Mike Jr. discovered that some of his money was missing. At the same time, Susan realized that the young couple had been using her credit cards. When she confronted them, reminding them of their agreement, an argument ensued. Andy and his girlfriend stormed out of the house.

"We assumed they would cool off and come back," Susan says. "But months passed and we had no word from them. Still, they were in the area—people would see them and call us. And when the baby was born at a nearby hospital, we sent flowers with a note: "We love you and want you in our lives." But Andy and his family did not respond. Eventually they dropped completely from sight. Mike asked a friend knowledgeable in finding people to track the couple, but after three months he reported failure. "Your son is either living far underground, maybe on the streets," the investigator told Mike, "or he's dead."

Susan and Mike had always had a network of supportive relatives and friends, mainly from their church community, St. Thomas of Villanova, in Palatine, Illinois. Now these friends reached out to the couple. As months passed with no word from Andy, people began to pray for him. Others attended morning mass on his behalf. Encouraging notes appeared in the Rheaumes' mailbox. At one point, during the second year of Andy's absence, a group held a prayer service for him, asking God to protect him and his family and bring them safely home.

Such support was critical to Mike and Susan, for by now their grief was profound. "When something like this happens, it's almost like going through a death, except that nothing ends," Susan says. "You worry, and imagine the worst. Is our son ill, or dead? Will we ever find our grandchild? You relive events from the past, asking yourself: What did we do wrong? Could we have prevented any of this?"

Mike wondered angrily why God was permitting this to happen to them. Hadn't they always done their best, for their children and for Him? Hadn't they prayed together faithfully, read and taught Scripture, made Him the center of their lives? Such questions were natural, Mike believes. But as months wore on, he came to the only conclusion he could: God was in charge, and God would see it all through.

As Christmas, 1994, approached, Mike began to believe that one more step was needed. Their close friends and family knew about Andy's absence, of course. But maybe *more* people should be praying. Andy's birthday was December 29. What if they asked not only their close friends, but their long-distance relatives, friends from long ago, and even business acquaintances—everyone on their Christmas card list—to pray for Andy on his birthday?

This was a risk, Mike knew, for it's difficult—in a world where everyone should "have it all together"—to expose one's wounds. Would people, confronted with their suffering, be uncomfortable with it? Would Mike and Susan be judged instead of consoled?

And yet, there is great power in prayer. If it could not banish Mike and Susan's sorrow, or bring them answers, perhaps it would provide the courage they needed to continue their lonely walk. After much thought, Mike inserted a little note in each Christmas card—"Please pray for Andy on December 29"—and dropped them all in the mail.

"The minute people received the cards, our phone began to ring," Susan recalls. "From everywhere, the universal response was: 'Why should we wait until Andy's birthday? We just wanted you to know we're praying *now.*'" It was a complete outpouring of love and acceptance, and as Christmas drew nearer, Susan and Mike felt sustained, even carried. Others, all across the country, every moment, were bearing their burden with them.

On the evening of December 23, as Susan's large extended family noisily arrived to begin the holidays, the phone rang. Mike answered it.

"Dad?" The voice on the other end was different, yet very familiar.

"Andy? Is it you?" Mike could hardly believe his ears. The hubbub in the room suddenly stopped.

"Yeah." There was a silence. "I live in California now."

Someone was running for Susan, telling her to pick up the extension. She did, but she couldn't talk. She could only weep.

Andy's relationship had crumbled, and he had sole custody of his daughter, Moriah, now three years old, who had cerebral palsy. He had also fathered two other children, in two other relationships, both of which had ended. Mike and Susan were somewhat stunned. This was not the news they had hoped to hear. Yet Andy was alive, and so was Moriah. During those lonely, agonizing nights of prayer, had they ever asked for more than this?

Mike made a quick decision. "Do you want to come home for Christmas, Andy?" he asked.

Susan, on the other phone, held her breath. "Yes," she heard her son say slowly. "I do."

They would arrange for plane tickets, Mike assured Andy, and pick him and Moriah up at the airport in twenty-four hours, on Christmas Eve. As he said good-bye, Mike had a final question. "Andy, it's been almost four years since we talked to you. Why did you call *now*?"

Another silence. "I don't know," Andy said.

Today Mike and Susan discuss their son and his life with evident relief, for he has moved back from California. But there is still sorrow mixed with the gladness, for Andy fathered still another child, a little boy born in 1996, who died tragically in an accident at six months of age. However, "Andy lives alone with his daughter, works at a home-based job, provides for Moriah's therapy, and, in some ways, manages very well," says Susan. There have been conflicts between parents and son, and Mike and Susan are still very concerned about the choices Andy has made, and the two grandchildren they've never met. But Moriah brings a special, unexpected joy. And the story hasn't ended yet.

"One of our friends, considering Andy's situation, laughed and said, 'Perhaps we should have prayed more specifically,'" Susan says. "But I believe that this is God's miracle. He started it, and He's going to finish it. Our job is to love and to pray, and to wait upon Him."

They won't be waiting alone. Andy may not know why he had that sudden impulse to phone his parents, but they do. They and the 124 families on their Christmas card list who gave the most important Christmas gift of all: faith.

The Ten Percent Solution

*Bring the whole tithe into the storehouse...and try me in this, says
the Lord of hosts: Shall I not open for you the flood-gates of heaven,
to pour down blessing upon you without measure?*

—MALACHI 3:10

ERVING THE LORD almost always involves going against the grain.
Often, the sacrifices or decisions we are called upon to make just
don't seem sensible. But these may be the very moments that, if we
choose God's way, can bring about the greatest blessings in our lives.

So it was with Clark Cothern. The son of a Southern Baptist pastor, Clark
grew up vowing he would never be one. "Not because my parents weren't
terrific," he says, "but I saw the heartache that is part of helping so many hurting
people," and he wanted no part of it. Instead, Clark prepared for a career in
music.

During his first year of college, he took a job in a small Phoenix, Arizona,
church as a part-time music director. Later, he toured America and Northern
Europe with a singing group, and saw many different styles of churches and
leadership. "This trip showed me that there were plenty of people just like me in
the ministry," he says. He also noticed that people in need were coming to him
for advice and prayer. Clark didn't feel his prayers were any more significant than

anyone else's, but he did the best he could. He got married, and with wife Joy's support served in several churches, usually as a music minister. After the birth of their second baby, the couple settled down in Ann Arbor, Michigan, not far from Joy's family. It was there that Clark's desire to become a pastor grew.

"Maybe it was the positive response I received from that wonderful congregation," he says, "or maybe it was just God's still small voice, nudging me to follow where He had been leading me all along." One day Clark announced to Joy that he believed not only that he should be a pastor, but that he should start a new church—in a place where people didn't usually attend church.

Joy was supportive of the idea, so she and Clark attended conferences, read books, and talked with others who had served as "home missionaries." Ironically, one of the prime places to start a church, they discovered, was in Phoenix, Arizona, where Clark had been raised. It would mean a whopping pay cut, and an uncertain outcome. But, filled with faith, the Cotherns made their plans.

Like many Christians, Clark and Joy had long been committed to the practice of tithing, that is, giving God ten percent of their earnings each month, usually via the collection basket at church. It was not that God needed their money, they knew; it was simply necessary for them to acknowledge that He was first in every area of their lives, even the material, and that they were completely dependent upon Him. Tithing was easy—the Cotherns didn't earn much, and they were used to being generous with their belongings and their time, as well as their cash. "Each time we moved, instead of carting all our furniture to a new location, we always gave some of it away, to people who had greater needs than we did," Clark explains. "But it wasn't that we were so saintly—we just couldn't see dragging stuff all over the country."

Now, preparing for Phoenix, they decided to give most of their furniture, including baby supplies, to an expectant couple in college. "Our two tots were still in diapers, but we felt that our family was complete, so others should get some use out of their clothes and equipment," Clark recalls. The college couple delightedly carted the huge load away. Only a few weeks later, Joy discovered she was expecting a third child.

"We were excited, but the timing was really tough on Joy," Clark says. "She was feeling pretty sick by the time we loaded our gear and headed west." Somewhat belatedly, Clark was realizing that obedience to God's call often costs the family more than it does the one who is being called. But once in Phoenix, he threw himself into his work—starting Bible study groups, writing pamphlets, and calling on potential church members. Joy was left in a overheated house—which sometimes reached 120 degrees during July—with two demanding toddlers and a pervasive worry over how they were going to provide for the new baby. Unpaid bills mounted, and no help came. What were they doing in this desert? Joy often wondered, as her little ones fussed and her back ached. Had they heard God's directions clearly? If so, why wasn't He providing for their needs?

Clark struggled with his own inadequacies. Some folks seemed less than enthusiastic about this fledgling church. Would he get it off the ground? Would he make enough money to support Joy and the children? Was he doing this for God, or for his own ego satisfaction? He found no answers anywhere.

One morning, as the baby's due date neared, things came to a head. It was time for Clark to write the monthly tithe check to the church. Instead, he threw his pen down on the table. Wasn't it a little ridiculous to give away some of their precious funds, then ask God to replenish the money so they could buy clothes and diapers? Why not just shortcut the process—keep the tithe money, and spend it on their newborn? It was logical, wasn't it? He turned to Joy. "I know that God always provides when we put Him first. But I'm so tired of hand-me-downs. Maybe I should use this money to buy some things you need."

Joy nodded, dispiritedly. "Just once I'd like to have something new. And I'd like our baby to wear a pretty outfit to the church's grand opening, instead of these stained leftovers." She sighed. "But if you think we should give the money to the church, it's fine with me."

Silence fell. How would God take care of their needs, if they didn't help Him do it? Yet if Clark didn't lead by example, how would those in his new congregation learn what faith really meant?

They looked at each other in wordless understanding. They had made a commitment, and they would stay the course. Slowly, Clark picked up the pen, wrote the tithe check, then looked at the balance that remained. Just enough for milk and bread until payday.

The following morning, a United Parcel Service truck pulled up in front of their house. The driver wrestled a huge box to the door. "There must be some mistake," Joy told him as she looked at the box's return address. "We don't know anyone in North Carolina."

The driver shrugged. "Is your name Cothern?"

"Yes."

"Then it's for you."

Puzzled, Joy signed the receipt. Clark came up behind her and looked at the box. "We don't know anyone in North Carolina," he told Joy.

"True," she said. "But I guess someone there knows us."

Clark got scissors, and opened the top. Just inside were snapshots, all of smiling strangers from a church congregation in North Carolina. Next to the pile was a note. "We called your mission board," it read. "We asked for the name and address of a missionary family about to have a baby, and they sent us yours. We hope you enjoy opening these things as much as we enjoyed wrapping them.

"Know that God cares for you, and we do too."

Joy started to cry. Because under the note were packages and packages and more packages all wrapped in baby shower paper, all—as she soon discovered—

containing items for their infant. God hadn't forgotten, after all. During the depths of their misery, He had already provided everything they would need.

Little Callie Elizabeth, born a few weeks later, was probably the prettiest girl at the church's successful grand opening. And amid all the excitement, the Cotherns pondered their miracle. Why had a North Carolina congregation felt led to supply strangers with a layette, instead of food or adult clothing or money? Surely there were other deserving mission families; why had the Cotherns been chosen? Perhaps most significant was the affirmation they had received, just when they needed it most: *Know that God cares for you, and we do too.* How had it all come about?

They never found the answers. But through the years, as the children grew, Clark's ministry flourished, and God provided many other examples of His love, the "baby box" became the symbol of it all. "Success isn't measured in dollars, but in how obedient we are to what we believe to be God's will," Clark says. "His purposes are often different from ours, because He's accomplishing things for eternity." But when His people step out in faith, they are blessed. Just ask the Cotherns.[6]

A Mother's Job

Love doesn't hide, it stays and fights. It goes the distance.
That's why God made love so strong.
So it can carry you, all the way home.

—MONICA
"Touched by an Angel"

WELVE YEARS AGO SUZAN KING* read a book, *The Helper,* written by Catherine Marshall, author of the beloved bestsellers *Christy* and *A Man Called Peter* among others. Catherine was a great believer in intercessory prayer, that is, when you pray on behalf of another person. At that time, Suzan was a self-described brand-new Christian. "I had been born and raised Lutheran—and if you'd asked me, I would have said I was a Christian," she explains. "But I didn't have a personal relationship with Jesus."

Recently, however, Suzan's life had become difficult. Her four daughters were teenagers, and there was turbulence in their home; one girl had moved out and another had run away. Suzan had medical problems too. One day, realizing that she was at the end of her rope, she had knelt in desperation. "Lord," she had prayed, "Come and take my life into your hands." And He had done so.

---

*All names in this story have been changed.

Now Suzan was reading books and looking for people to help her develop in this new and deeper walk. "Gradually, He brought godly women into my life, and when they saw my desire to get closer to Him, they began to disciple me," Suzan says. One in particular taught her more about intercessory prayer. Gradually, Suzan felt God was calling her to pray in this way.

She began during her morning walks. There was something about the air, the scents and sights of nature, that allowed her to feel close to God. She prayed primarily for the daughter who had run away, asking that God keep her safe and bring her back. But soon another family problem loomed. One morning her second-oldest, Charlotte, told Suzan that Beth, the youngest, was planning a secret date that evening with a boy she knew Mom and Dad would not like.

"Tom and I had always insisted we meet and approve any boy our daughters dated," Suzan explains. "Beth was obviously breaking that rule."

After breakfast, Suzan immediately went for her walk. "God," she prayed, "if Tom and I confront Beth about this, she might defy us, or worse, move out. I don't think I could survive that again, with another daughter. But if we don't say anything, she'll get away with it. How should I pray for her? What shall I ask?"

Suzan waited a moment. Was it her imagination, or did she hear specific words moving in her heart? *Pray for intervention,* the message said.

Intervention...Didn't that mean asking God to take control of the whole situation? This was chancy. But Suzan was in a foxhole, with no other answers in sight. And she knew God respected her free will enough to wait until He was asked. "God, please intervene," she prayed. "Work your will in this situation."

Immediately she was flooded with peace. She had done what He requested, and the rest was up to Him.

As evening approached, Suzan behaved as if nothing were amiss. What would God do, she wondered? How would He resolve the situation? Or was it going to be resolved? Perhaps she would have to stand by and watch Beth actually leave, pretending that she did not know about the secret date. Could she do it? She had thought she might be tempted to take the problem back from Him, to confront Beth after all. But oddly, she remained calm. "It was," she says, "as if the Holy Spirit had given me a supernatural gift of faith."

A few hours before the date, Beth came home unexpectedly from her after-school job. "I've got a terrible toothache," she told her mother. "I made a dentist appointment for tomorrow, but I'm going to bed now." Suzan was amazed. Beth had never had a toothache before (nor has she had once since). But the secret date had obviously been canceled.

The following Friday, however, Charlotte told Suzan that the date was on again, for Saturday right after work. "God," Suzan asked, "what should I do this time?"

Again the unmistakable answer came. *Pray for intervention.* Suzan did. She was almost not surprised when Beth got ready to leave for work on Saturday morning, and discovered that her car battery was dead. "I guess Dad will have to drive you and pick you up from work today," Suzan told her daughter. Beth nodded glumly. Another plan foiled!

Beth made another secret plan, and another. In every case, her mother prayed for intervention. In every case, the plan failed. Eventually, since they were never able to go out together, Beth lost interest in the boy. "The most amazing part about it all was that none of the circumstances obstructing Beth's plans had any direct connection with her dad or me," Suzan says. "So we were able to keep our already—fragile relationship intact."

Through the next several years, Tom and Suzan deepened their relationships with all their daughters. One December morning during her senior year in college, however, Beth phoned. "I'm not coming home for the holidays, Mom," she announced.

"But why?" Suzan was shocked. Their oldest daughter was bringing her new baby home for Christmas, and the family was looking forward to being together.

"I'm going to South Dakota to spend Christmas with my roommate's family," Beth explained.

"Well, if that's what you really want..." Suzan stayed calm. But as soon as she hung up she began the familiar pattern of prayer. "God, please intervene," she asked. "Work out your will for Beth over the holidays. If you want her to go to South Dakota, I won't get in your way."

God did not want Beth to go to South Dakota. Suzan felt it immediately. In fact, Suzan was certain that Beth had a "divine appointment" already scheduled here at home.

Of course she said nothing to Beth when they spoke the following week. "I'm working out the plans for South Dakota," Beth told her mother confidently. "And if I can't get a flight, I just met a boy who's driving there, and he says I can ride along."

A boy she barely knew... And what if the weather turned dangerous? Suzan remained noncommittal. But after the call, she stormed heaven again—just in case God had been occupied elsewhere!

The following week, Beth called again. "Mom, I can't believe it! I couldn't get a ticket on any flight—they're all booked. And that driver canceled too. No matter what arrangements I try to make, they all fall through!" Beth paused suspiciously as a thought occurred to her. "Mom, do you know anything about this?"

Suzan smiled. The girls were catching on to her heavenly pipeline. "Honey, I just think you're supposed to be here."

"Well, I'm giving up. I'll be home for Christmas."

It was the best gift Suzan would receive. But there was more in store. That week, a Christian organization in the area arranged a party for the college sons and daughters of those who worked with them. And when Beth attended, she met a young man named John. John's parents were missionaries, and the entire family had just returned from an assignment on the other side of the world. Interestingly, Beth's dad knew John's dad, and the two had talked about how compatible their children might be.

"John had grown up overseas, thousands of miles from where we lived," Suzan says. "But God arranged for him to come to our town at just the right time to meet Beth, a girl he never would have met had she gone to South Dakota that Christmas."

The families were delighted but not really surprised when John and Beth married in 1990. Nor has Suzan been surprised to learn that the couple pray over their little son, Philip, all the time. They ask God to intervene, to let Philip know Jesus at an early age, and to find their son a godly woman when the time is right. And why not? John and Beth have learned from an "expert" that life works best when we let God take charge.

That's What Friends Are For

No man is a failure who has friends.
—It's a Wonderful Life

ON JOHNSON WAS DELIGHTED. He had just paid off the mortgage on his duplex in Salt Lake City. Now he no longer needed the rental income from the second unit, so he could follow a long-time dream: remodeling the building into one wonderful house.

Ron hadn't contracted for any of the work yet when he discovered that Joe, one of his friends, needed an apartment. "I had met Joe when I was teaching country dancing," Ron recalls. "He was a quick learner and really enjoyed himself. People liked him a lot." The duplex remodeling could wait, Ron thought, and he offered to rent the vacant apartment to Joe. Joe gratefully accepted.

Landlord and tenant got along well. "Joe was an auto mechanic, with an amazing ability to use his common sense to figure things out," Ron says. He knew that Joe had been divorced some years back, and had two children and several siblings, but that family ties seemed loose; when Joe hosted a party to celebrate his parents' fiftieth wedding anniversary, for example, some of his brothers and sisters didn't attend. Nor did Joe's children visit very often. Joe didn't talk much about his family situation, however, and Ron respected his privacy.

Besides, he was busy enough with his sign business, located next-door to his duplex, as well as his involvement in several community organizations. And when Christmas rolled around each year, Ron was a self-described "yuletide lunatic," displaying trimmed trees, a Nativity scene, a holiday village, and many other decorations both inside and out. "Mine is one of those houses that stop traffic, and is always on the newspaper's list of 'places to see,'" he explains. That Christmas, Joe got into the spirit too, building several animated characters and, with Ron, a marvelous miniature carousel.

"You know," he told Ron one night, "you've rekindled my love of this season. I guess I'd lost the meaning of it all during some difficult times. But it's back."

Joe had lived in the duplex for just over a year when he suffered a seizure, and was told he had a terminal illness. It was a tremendous blow. "Yet Joe was determined to fight, and not let anything ruin whatever time he had left," Ron says. Soon environmental conditions at the garage where Joe worked aggravated his illness, and he had to quit his job. His income dropped drastically, and he could no longer afford to rent Ron's apartment.

"You've been planning to remodel it anyway," Joe told Ron one evening. "If I move out, you can start the work now."

"But where would you go?" Ron asked, still shocked at this turn of events. To date, he knew, none of Joe's relatives had offered help.

Joe shrugged. Did his living arrangements really matter, at this point?

To Ron, they did. "You'll stay in the apartment, rent-free," he told Joe firmly. "But..."

"Rent-free. And I don't want to hear another word about it."

Joe agreed, on the condition that Ron would allow him to start the planned renovations. When Ron protested that the work would be too demanding, Joe assured him that it would not. "Besides," he pointed out, "it's a way that I can give something back to you, to thank you for..." He stopped. Words had failed him. And so Ron relented.

Joe started treatment, and together the men began remodeling. Over the next months, as Joe delightedly showed interested visitors the changes he was making on the house, his health improved. In November 1994, when Joe performed in a country dancing show at the University of Utah, and later put up Ron's huge outdoor Christmas display, his illness seemed almost a thing of the past. But in January, doctors discovered a brain tumor. Joe's time was running out.

Ron refused to put Joe in a nursing home for his final days, despite paralysis on his right side and other difficult symptoms. Instead, he rented a hospital bed for his home, and alerted Joe's friends. With their help, and visits from hospice nurses and Joe's two children, Joe stayed in the house where he had enjoyed life so much. "A few of Joe's relatives came to see him during the last week or so," Ron says. "For some, it was the first time. But when Joe died, a friend and I were the only ones with him. Sally was holding his left hand, and I his right. At the moment of death, I became aware of a movement up the wall near his head, as if his spirit was leaving his body. Then, with his paralyzed hand, he squeezed mine, in a firm grip." An involuntary motion? Perhaps. But Sally, holding Joe's good hand, felt nothing at all. "I thought then, and still do," says Ron, "that it was his way of thanking me for my help, and letting me know that everything was okay."

Because Joe's financial situation had been precarious, he had prepaid some of his final expenses, but not enough. And although his relatives had assured Ron they would cover any additional costs, no one actually volunteered when the money was finally needed. So Ron arranged the funeral and signed papers making him legally responsible for the remaining charges. It was, he felt, his last act of commitment. He had forfeited rent money, and would spend more at the mortuary—and maybe some folks thought he was a fool. But hadn't Jesus pointed out that the greatest of all loves was to lay down one's life (and presumably one's material goods) for a friend?

Word about Ron's generosity got around, and checks from Joe's friends started coming into the funeral home. By the time Ron received the final bill, it had been cut to $1,393. Still a sacrifice for him, but Ron paid it promptly, and closed a chapter in his life.

He thought.

One evening the following summer, Ron was working in his garden. As he finished putting fertilizer on the last plant, he heard a command in his mind: *Take the fertilizer bag to the garage.*

Ron paused. Why would he do that? He always stored fertilizer off the patio, much closer to the garden. Again, he heard the voice: *Take the bag to the garage.* Ron obeyed.

At the same moment, a friend of Ron's, who had stopped by, came up the basement stairs. He too heard a voice: *You dropped your checkbook. Go back for it.* Instantly, the friend turned and went down the stairs.

Just then, a gust of wind broke a huge limb from a tree behind the garage and sent it crashing across the patio and through the open basement door, right where the men had been. "Only later did the 'shakes' hit," Ron says. "I realized that if we hadn't heeded those warnings, we surely would have been killed."

Despite having carried homeowner's insurance for twenty-two years, Ron had never had a claim, and he didn't know if such damage would be covered. He called the company, and a representative came out. "The tree needs to be cut up," Ron explained, "and the wall replaced, and the hole in the deck patched." The adjuster nodded and left.

Weeks passed, and Ron heard nothing from the company. Assuming the claim had been denied, he decided to hire people to do the work. His brother, however, had a chain saw. "We can cut those limbs ourselves," he told Ron. They did. Once they hauled the mess away, Ron realized that, although he rarely kept such products on hand, he had just enough of the perfect patching material to fix the hole himself rather than hire a professional. And instead of replacing the damaged wall, he tore it out. It was back-breaking, time-consuming work, but the new area looked even better than it had before.

Shortly after the repairs were done, Ron received a letter from the insurance company. There was no itemized bill included to show just how the company had arrived at its total, just an explanation that the enclosed check should reimburse him for his property damages. They hadn't denied the claim after all! Pleased, Ron looked at the check, and a chill ran through him. It was made out for $1,393—the exact amount he had spent on Joe's funeral four months before.

The memories came to him: Joe homeless, ill, lonely… Ron doing his best to help, because he could imagine no other course. Now, with utter certainty, he knew. This check, this entire rescue in the yard, wasn't a coincidence at all. While he had been watching out for his friend, God had been watching out for him.

Ron now opens his refurbished, decorated house for Christmas tours each year to raise money for charity, in memory of Joe. Moreover, visitors love the animated carousel the two men built so much that Ron now makes others to sell, an unexpected side business from this unexpected adventure.

"I've never been real religious, but I've always believed there was 'something else,' Ron says today. "Now I believe that we're all here for a specific reason. We have lessons to learn, and things we need to teach others by our example. There is much more to life than the 'reality' we see around us."[7]

Over the Hills, and Everywhere

*The people who walked in darkness have
seen a great light; Upon those who dwelt
in the land of gloom a light has shone.*

—ISAIAH 9:1

BUD AND JANE SURBER OF SALIDA, COLORADO, are a remarkable couple. They've raised seven children and taken in sixty foster children, and now enjoy frequent visits from twenty-one grandchildren, all on their large ranch which lies at the bottom of a hill known as Angel Mountain. The name is fitting, for angels have played a considerable role in keeping their large brood well and happy, Jane and Bud believe, and in bringing other blessings too. The wooden cross overlooking their property is a constant reminder of that.

The cross was constructed years ago when several of the Surber youngsters were members of a 4-H Club. For a project, they had to build something that the entire community would enjoy. Since Angel Mountain was directly behind them, the kids decided to make a cross, which would be visible from the road as their neighbors drove by. Using a scaffold, Bud helped the kids form the cross out of two huge telephone poles. But it needed something more. "I know!" one of the boys said. "Let's put lights on it, so people can see it at night!"

This was a bit more complicated. But since Bud was an electrician for Public Service Company of Colorado, he knew how to tap electric power from the house. He built a junction box, added an extension wire, and connected the other end to several long fluorescent tubes, which the children mounted on the poles. The first night they turned it on, the family stared in awe. It was beautiful, glorious, like a huge heavenly star. Their neighbors, and travelers passing on Highway 285, would see it too. What a wonderful way to announce Christmas!

The Surbers lit the cross each night during that first holiday season, and continued through January. Everyone appreciated it. One morning Jane walked down to the mailbox and found a note from a long-distance trucker. "I had been contemplating suicide for a while," he wrote, "and then, from a far-off distance, I saw your cross. I followed the light all across the plains, and by the time I got here, I had changed my mind. Your cross gave me the hope I needed to go on."

Jane and Bud were thrilled that the children's project had actually saved a life. But at the end of January, they received a rude awakening. The electric bill arrived, and due to the cross, "it had skyrocketed," Jane recalls. "We knew we couldn't afford to turn the cross on every night anymore, so we decided to save it for special occasions." And so they did. Whenever they lighted it, travelers who were lost or experiencing car trouble invariably turned in at their gates. "I guess they figured any family with a lighted cross on their property would be willing to help them out," Jane says. "We met a lot of nice people that way."

Years passed. Some of the children married and moved to other areas. Bud was transferred too. His mother stayed on the ranch—it had been in their family for over one hundred years—but he, Jane, and the remaining children left Salida. By this time, the cross had fallen into disrepair, and hadn't been turned on for several years. Lightning had struck it more than once, and the little connectors between the fluorescent tubes had cracked and rusted, breaking the flow of power. Bud never considered dismantling the cross—he still remembered the care and love the children had put into it. But obviously its importance had come to an end.

In 1989 Bud retired, and he, Jane, their two youngest sons, and four foster daughters returned to the ranch. Shortly afterward, one of their sons-in-law died suddenly. "It was a tragic time, especially for our widowed daughter, Gail, and her children," Jane says. Gail and her children moved back to the ranch, where the family wrapped them in love and support. But Christmas was fast approaching. How would they get through it this year?

December 24 dawned, and children, in-laws, and grandchildren began to arrive, presents in tow. Despite the laughter and camaraderie, everyone was uncomfortably aware of Gail's pain. If only they could do something special for her, something to make this Christmas a little more bearable! But what?

Jane knew their feelings and felt the same way. "Gail," she asked, as the others milled around the kitchen, making breakfast, mixing cookie dough, and planning their day together, "is there anything any of us can do for you?"

Gail paused. "I wish...

"Yes?" The kitchen suddenly became very quiet.

"I wish we could light the cross tonight."

Her siblings looked at each other, then at Bud. The cross. Everyone knew it had deteriorated completely. It had been years since they had even thought about it, much less checked to see if it could be restored. Worse, the weather was bitterly cold, with a terrible mountain wind that would make outdoor work even harsher than usual.

But love, real love, never counts the cost. Immediately, everyone reached for jackets and scarves, united in a common cause. If a lighted cross would bring memories of an earlier, happier time to Gail, if it would heal her even for a moment, it was worth trying.

"Our kids, in-law kids, and foster daughters labored outside all day," Jane recalls. Some climbed the high crossbar; others attempted, with frozen fingers, to coax rusted parts to function. Nothing worked.

Jane couldn't see much from the kitchen, but as hours passed with no triumphant shouts, she began to worry. In late afternoon she noticed, with a sinking heart, that snow had begun to fall. Soon darkness descended, and a son stomped in to get some flashlights. "Anything happening?" Jane asked him.

He looked at her through iced—up eyelashes, his face raw from the wind. "It's impossible, Mom," he said, slamming the door behind him.

Another hour passed. Finally Jane threw on a coat and went outside. She could see flashlight beams still moving on the hill, but the cross remained dark. Bud was walking slowly toward the house, and she ran to meet him. "No chance?" she asked quietly.

"None." He sighed and put an arm around her. "As soon as one wire's repaired, we find another broken one. There's no end to it. It would take a miracle to help us now."

A miracle. *That's* what Gail needed, and what her family was feverishly working to give her, Jane realized. Not just a lighted cross, but a sign that she would survive this terrible loss, that life would be good again someday. And weren't miracles what Christmas was all about? "Lord Jesus, send us a miracle," Jane prayed. "Show us your love in a special way tonight."

They had reached the house and now, heartsick and frustrated, Bud moved away from Jane. He looked for a moment at the junction box that linked the cross's useless wires to the power source. And then, with one booted foot, he kicked it.

A huge cheer suddenly erupted from the hill. Jane turned first. "Bud, look!" she exclaimed. The cross was shining bright.

It was a good Christmas that year, despite the underlying grief. And Gail was perhaps the most hopeful of all. God had sent her a message through her family that she was surrounded with love, and that He would never abandon her. Although she didn't yet know how she would manage, the answers would surely come. The family too was joyful. They had sacrificed their comfort for what seemed a desperate cause, and God had rewarded their efforts as well.

The cross continued to glow each night, again a beacon not only for the Surbers but for everyone traveling along the highway. And it could burn forever, as far as Jane was concerned; a huge electric bill would be a small price to pay for the memory of that renewed hope in her daughter's eyes. But it wasn't until the January bill came that Jane realized the full extent of their Christmas gift. For despite the constant use of extra power, there was no change at all in the bill. It showed the same amount due as always. "How could this be?" Jane asked Bud.

He didn't know. Nor had he been able to figure out just why the cross was turning on automatically each evening. For despite his kick to the junction box that Christmas Eve, several of the connectors on the poles were still broken. And the timer that he had installed after Christmas, he had just discovered, had split in two because of the frost. There was no way that electricity could be reaching that cross.

No earthly way, that is.

But if you're ever on Colorado's Highway 285 and you pass a cross glowing brightly on Angel Mountain, you might want to stop for just a moment or two. Surely there are miracles there, as in all places that He has touched. And you might even hear the echo of those long-ago heavenly hosts, singing the same marvelous message:

"Glory to God in the highest, and peace on earth to those on whom His favor rests."

What a blessing. For then, for now, forever.

～ *Notes* ～

1. A few Christmases after he brought toys to the Thills, Tom Daly became ill. Only a double transplant—liver and kidney—could save him, and there was no donor to be found. On a cold January day, Tom's physician informed the family that unless a "miracle donor" emerged, Tom would not last through the night. They gathered around his bedside to prepare for the final parting.

    To their astonishment, before the day ended, a "miracle donor"—a perfect match—became available. Tom was rushed into surgery. He returned to work in two months, and enjoys a healthy, fulfilling life today.

    "My wife has always believed that someone brought a blessing to me because I brought blessings to the Thills and others," he says. "'Bread upon the waters' is more than just a nice idea. It works."

2. Kimberley Griffiths Little has just published her first book, for middle-grade children: *Break-Away* (Avon) is the story of a twelve-year-old who makes his dreams of playing soccer come true against great odds.

3. This book is *The Christmas Menorahs: How a Town Fought Hate*, by Janice Cohn, published in 1995 by Albert Whitman and Company, Morton Grove, IL 60053.

4. Bonnie (not her real name) told me this story at my book-signing table after I had given a talk on angels. There were a lot of people milling about, and I neglected to get her name. Perhaps she will read this, and contact me.

5. Kidney transplants are not as risky now as they were in the mid-1980s, when Donna and Ray went through their surgeries. New drugs help recipients accept transplants more easily. Donors face no lifestyle restrictions

after the operation, and their one remaining kidney is able to do the work of two. Since eight people in the United States die each day while waiting for a new kidney, it makes sense for everyone to fill out a driver's license donor card, to be used after death.

6. Clark Cothern is working on a new book about fatherhood, soon to be published by Questar.

7. If you would like information about Ron Johnson's custom—built Christmas Carousels, you can contact him at Carnival Classics, 1414 South West Temple, Salt Lake City, UT 84115, or fax: 801-466-5344.

~ *Afterword* ~

I AM ALWAYS INTERESTED in hearing from readers who would like to share their angel encounters, miracles, answers to prayer, and other heavenly wonders. Please write to me at P.O. Box 127, Prospect Heights, IL 60070. Or you can e-mail me at angelwak@mcs.com or visit my Web site at http://www.mcs.net/~angelwak/home.html.

If I can use your story in my future writing, I will contact you for permission.

—JOAN WESTER ANDERSON

Christmas Angels
All Year Round

Christmas Miracles

Christmas
Miracles

Magical True Stories
of Modern-Day Miracles

JAMIE C. MILLER,
LAURA LEWIS, AND
JENNIFER BASYE SANDER

CARMEL • NEW YORK 10512

This Guideposts edition is published by special arrangementwith William Morrow and Company, Inc.

Library of Congress Cataloging-in-Publication Data

Christmas miracles : magical true stories of modern-day miracles /
Jamie C. Miller, Laura Lewis, and Jennifer Basye Sander

p. cm.

ISBN 0-688-15588-X

1. Miracles.   2. Christmas.   3. Religious biography.   I. Miller, Jamie C.
II. Lewis, Laura, 1963–   .   III. Sander, Jennifer Basye, 1958–
BT97.2.C455   1997
242'.355—dc21   97.15524
                                                    CIP

http://www.guideposts.org.
Designed by José R. Fonfrias
Typeset by Composition Technologies, Inc.
Printed in the United States of America

To Julian, Evan, Olivia, Alex, Ian, Kelly, Seth, and Ryan
Our own miracles

Contents

INTRODUCTION   3

Christmas Loaves and Fishes   5
Raynier Maharaj

Christmas Saved My Mother's Life   8
Rabbi Abie Ingber

The Stranger   11
Kerstin Backman

O Christmas Tree   18
Jannis Gardner

Chester   23
John Emery

One Last Wish   27
Cynthia Stewart-Copier

Bologna from Heaven   33
Nora Lynn

Contents

The Town That Gave Christmas 37
Marian Jeppson Walker

Merry Christmas, Mrs. Moring 43
Allyson Moring

Icy Water Rescue 49
Holly DeGroot

The Gold and Ivory Tablecloth 52
Rev. Howard C. Schade

Second Chance 56
Isaiah McKinnon

The Kiss 59
Olivia Pratt

The Gift 63
Miki Hsu Leavey

Ten-Candy-Bar Christmas 66
Cathe Odom

Homeless Santa 69
Jennifer Basye Sander

Contents

The Secret Dolls 72
MarGene B. Lyon

My Shiny Fire Truck 75
Kit Dillon Givas

Circle of Love 78
Valerie J. Reynoso

Christmas Doesn't Come from a Store 83
Sandi Schureman

An All-American Christmas 86
Cathy Caldwell

First Christmas 90
Kristen Gurksnis

My Christmas Angel 95
Ron Brand

The Story of Punkin and Boo 99
Molly Furman

Exchange of Gifts 102
Wendy Thayer Gallagher

Contents

The Riches of Family   105
Donna King Conkling

The Silver Star   110
Ivan T. Anderson

A Glimpse of Christmas   113
Marlena de Blasi

The Good Samaritans   117
Susie Wagner

The Sacrifice   120
Aney B. Chatterton

A Miracle Touched My Life   125
Marianna Shugart Laney

Someone to Watch Over Me   128
Dianne Campbell-Ostdiek

ACKNOWLEDGMENTS   133

Christmas Miracles

❦ *Introduction* ❧

miracle n. *1. An event that seems impossible to explain by natural laws and so is regarded as supernatural in origin or as an act of God. 2. One that excites admiration or awe.*

Webster's II New Riverside Dictionary

EACH YEAR AT CHRISTMAS even the most jaded hearts are softened by reports of wondrous occurrences, from unlikely reunions to dramatic medical recoveries, from newly formed romances to the sudden reappearance of long-lost possessions. Why should these things happen then, and why do we feel so touched by them?

During the Christmas season all people the world over are looking for miracles, opening their hearts to the possibility of a miracle for just a few short weeks. World-weary souls soften and become open windows through which miraculous deeds can fly and happen upon the unwary, who might shut them out at other times of the year. Churchgoers sit amid hundreds of flickering candles at midnight services, remembering an ancient pilgrimage to a stable and a star, awed by the beauty of the sight and ready to see an angel on the road that night. Tired shoppers drag home from yet another crowded mall, disheartened by the season's commercialism and willing to see a miracle in the small gesture of a stranger. Miracles big and small happen every day during Christmastime—if we are open and receptive to them.

In the pages of *Christmas Miracles* you will find true stories of miraculous occurrences that happened to folks just like you: small, sweet stories of remarkable events that happened on or near Christmas. You will read of those who are suddenly willing to stoop down and consider the needs or desires of little children; people who remember the weaknesses and loneliness of the elderly; folks who, if only for one short season, stop asking how much their friends love them and instead wonder how much love they can show to their friends.

We three editors all come from families with strong storytelling traditions, and no night is a better night for stories than Christmas Eve. After the dinner dishes were cleared away and the small children sent up to bed, we listened late into the night as our parents and grandparents told old family stories like that of the young doctor's all-night walk home alone through the countryside on Christmas night after saving the life of a farm boy, the father's payment of a dozen fresh eggs carefully cradled in his black medical bag, or the Swedish folkrale about the bear who saves the life of a wealthy landowner, only to lose his own life in return. And so one night when we found ourselves sharing these stories together, we realized that there must be a wider audience for these true tales of Christmas miracles. May you and your family enjoy each story and may you bask in their glow for the year to come.

Albert Einstein said, "There are only two ways to live your life. One is as though nothing is a miracle. The other is as if everything is." It is our hope that the stories in *Christmas Miracles* weave the magic of brotherhood, fill hearts with peace, and cause a frightened world to pause—to remember—and to hope. As you read these stories, keep your eyes open, keep your heart open, and let the miracles begin.

Christmas Loaves
and Fishes

N CHRISTMAS EVE in homes everywhere, there is quiet excitement. The festive feeling and the warmth of having family near brings to mind a Christmas tale I love to relate each year. It's a true story, even though it might sound unbelievable. And it gives proof that miracles do happen.

A long time ago there was a group of young people who decided to spread some Christmas cheer. They had discovered that there were several children who would be spending the festive day in a community hospital nearby. So they bought nice presents, wrapped them and, armed with guitars, sweet voices and one of the friends dressed as Santa Claus, dropped in unexpectedly at the hospital on Christmas Eve.

The children were overjoyed at seeing Santa, and by the time the group was finished handing our presents and singing Christmas carols, there were tears in everyone's eyes. From then on, it was decided they would play Santa every year.

The following Christmas Eve, the ladies at the hospital were included in the rounds, and by the third year it was expanded to embrace some poor children in the neighborhood.

On the fourth Christmas Eve, however, after all the rounds were made, Santa

Claus looked into his bag and discovered there were a few extra toys left. So the friends mulled it over, trying to figure out what to do with them. Somebody mentioned that there were a few squatters' shacks nearby in which a couple of desperately poor families lived.

So the group decided to go there, thinking there were perhaps three families at most. But as they drove over the crest of the hill into this lonely area—it was around midnight now—the shocked group saw a large number of people standing at the side of the street.

They were children—more than thirty of them. Behind them were not three shacks but rows and rows of shabby squatters' dwellings. As the cars drew to a stop, the children came running up, shouting with joy. It turned out they had been waiting patiently all night for Santa Claus. Somebody—no one could remember who—had told them he was coming, although *our* Santa had decided to go there only moments before.

Everyone was stunned, except for Santa. He was in a panic. He knew he didn't have enough toys for all these kids. Eventually, not wanting to disappoint the children, he decided to give whatever toys he had only to the smallest children. When the presents ran our, he'd just have to explain to the bigger kids what had happened.

So moments later he found himself perched on top of a car s hood as these thirty or more sparkling clean children, dressed in their best clothes, lined up in order of height, with the smallest first, for their moment with him. As each anxious child approached, Santa dipped into his bag, his heart heavy with dread, hoping to find at least one more toy. And, by some miracle, he found one each time he dipped. And as the last of the children received a present, Santa looked into the now deflated bag. It was empty—empty as it should have been twenty-four children ago.

With relief, he let our a hearty "Ho ho ho" and bade the kids farewell. But as he was about to enter the car (the reindeer, apparently, had the day off), he heard a child scream, "Santa! Santa! Wait!" And out of the bushes rushed two little children, a boy and a girl. They had been asleep.

Santa's heart sank. This time he knew for sure he had no more toys. The bag was empty. But as the out-of-breath kids approached, he summoned up some courage and dipped into the bag once more. And, lo and behold, there were two more presents in there.

The group of friends, now all grown adults, still talk about this miracle on Christmas morning. They still have no explanation for it, other than the fact that it happened. How do I know so much about this? Well, I was the one playing Santa.

RAYNIER MAHARAJ
Toronto, Canada

Christmas Saved
My Mother's Life

NY STUDENT OF THE TWENTIETH CENTURY would affirm that the Holocaust was one of the darkest chapters of modern history. Yet within that nightmare, there were moments of humanity and life-giving compassion.

In August of 1942 my mother, Fania Paszt, was one of the last survivors of the Lutsk ghetto in Poland. She was a young girl, not yet twenty years old, when her life was saved by the miraculous appearance of one righteous Christian after another. No one could ever know why she was spared and her parents, her brothers, and other family members were so brutally murdered. Evangelical Christians, farmers and peasants each arrived at a precise life-saving moment to hide her in attics, cellars, and chicken coops.

My mother's Christmas miracle began on August 19, 1942, when a Ukrainian peasant came into the ghetto and proposed a plan to hide my mother's family in the town. Not wanting to jeopardize her entire family with a risky plan, my mother tore off the yellow Star of David patch that she was required to display as a Jew, covered her head with a shawl, and, leaving behind her entire family, set out with the peasant to test the escape route. Luck was with them, and she was able to slip out from the ghetto without being stopped by the unusually large number of Ukrainian police and German soldiers gathered on its edges. The plan was to return the next morning and smuggle her entire family out with her. However, as she approached the ghetto the next day, she was stopped by a Ukrainian policeman. Taking her for a fellow Christian, not a Jew, he warned her away from the area. "It has been sealed off for official reasons."

Jews had lived in Lutsk since the tenth century and had flourished with the city as it became a political and economic center in the mid-sixteenth century. But on the morning of August 20, the day my mother stood outside the ghetto, an order had been given to end that history once and for all. Over the course of the next two days, seventeen thousand Jews from the Lutsk ghetto were led to the Polanka Hill on the outskirts of the city, thrown live into pits, and machine-gunned to death. Every Jew found within the borders of the ghetto was murdered.

My mother's brave expedition out of the ghetto had saved her. Having lost everything and everyone, my dazed mother returned to her guide's home and spent the next few months hidden in the flue of his outdoor country oven.

But on December 24, 1942, Fania Paszt's luck seemed to run out. The Ukrainian peasant who had saved her life feared for his own safety should he continue to harbor her, and turned her out of his house. My mother wandered the dirt roads of the countryside, freezing cold in her tattered cotton dress. As night descended, she knew her life was at its end. Recognizing the manor house of the county warden, she turned up its path. The warden's dogs jumped on her, ripped her dress, and bit her. The warden, hearing the commotion of the dogs, appeared at his door with a gun in his hand.

"Please shoot me," my mother begged. "Let me share the fate of my family." "I cannot kill you tonight," responded the official. He took her inside, fed her some of his own family's Christmas Eve dinner, and gave her a new dress and a place to sleep for the night. The next morning, fearful that he could be killed for saving a Jew, he took her into town and gave her over to another Christian family to hide. Three more Christians magically stepped forward during the war to save her life until the day she descended from an attic during the Russian liberation of Lutsk in 1944. She was one of the few Jews still alive in the town.

Only decades later did I learn of the Polish expression, "On Christmas Eve, even a stray cat is allowed to live." On the evening of December 24, 1942, my mother had been like a stray cat in the Polish countryside. At that precise moment, God had to invoke Christmas Eve to save her life. I am proud of my Jewish heritage and of my calling as a rabbi, but I will never forget the legacy that Christmas saved my mother's life. "Merry Christmas to all," from a grateful rabbi.

—RABBI ABIE INGBER
Cincinnati, Ohio

The Stranger

T WAS CHRISTMAS EVE twenty years ago, the very first Christmas we spent in our small, red wooden farmhouse on the outskirts of a forest in the north of Sweden. The place was old and very old-fashioned but so cheap that we could afford it. It had a small stable where we could keep a few horses and two small fields for the horses to run in. A narrow road led out to the main road. We were so far from the closest town that ours was always one of the last roads to be cleared of snow.

This Christmas seemed magical to us. Our family had never lived in the country before. Snow had been falling for days and the whole world was white and soft with downy snow. The neighborhood looked like a frozen sea with giant white frozen waves. Late on that day, the snow stopped falling and the clouds vanished slowly. Pale sunshine from the sinking sun was reflected in sparkling cascades on the snow. The birches and pine trees in the forest were furry with snow.

It was like living in one of those glittering Christmas cards, and we were childishly happy in the silent whiteness. This winter seemed like a special gift made exclusively for us. Along with my husband and our two young children, I felt that this was a Christmas when anything could happen.

We had our traditional Christmas dinner late in the day, gathered around our old kitchen table. It was a traditional Swedish holiday dinner—a big ham, ribs, cabbage, and peas, served with breads, cheeses, and sausages of all kinds.

Afterward we sat talking together in the flickering candlelight in the small sitting room and ignored the piles of dirty dishes in the kitchen.

Just then—at half past ten on a pitch-dark Christmas night—someone pounded on our front door.

We looked at each other around the table. We did not yet know any of our new neighbors, and of our old friends, who could possibly be dropping in on us, given that we lived so far from town? Another knock sounded. I got up and went to see who it was.

There in the snow, quite alone and with a sparkling, star-studded sky shining behind him, stood a complete stranger. On this cold Swedish night he wore no hat. His soft blond hair formed a halo around his head, his breath grew like a cloud our of his half-open mouth, and a pair of big eyes shone in a very pale face.

I stared at him. Then I looked out into the yard beyond him to see if anyone was with him. The yard was empty. All I could see was the deep, black holes in the snow that marked his path up to the front door.

He just stood there as I looked at him, his hands in his pockets, watching me. At last he spoke.

"Excuse me, ma'am, but have you got a television set?"

His question was so unexpected that I did not quite know what to say.

"Ah, well, yes...yes we have," I said.

"Could you possibly let me watch a television program? I think there is one I'd like to see." His voice was soft and friendly. I stood silent. My first thought was that I must say no in the politest way possible. But although my mind thought of refusal, my tongue refused to say no. Deep inside I seemed to hear the voice of my pious old grandfather telling me, "The Christmas night is holy. You must never turn anyone away from your house that night, for if you do you are turning away Christ."

"Well…" I said slowly, trying to .think of what to do. "What program would that be?"

"I don't remember," he said, "but if you will let me look in the newspaper I will tell you which one."

"Maybe you had better come in," I said, and opened the door the rest of the way.

The young man walked up the three steps and held out his hand for a firm handshake. He did not say what his name was and I did not ask. His hand was icy cold and I quickly saw the reason why: He had no mittens on. He was dressed in a worn gray trench coat buttoned up to his chin and he wore big rubber boots. Not much to wear on a cold winter night, I said to myself.

His eyes were blue like the summer sky, and when he smiled, I was surprised to see the trust in his eyes and on his face. I got the distinct feeling that he had been certain that I would let him in.

I invited him into the warm kitchen. As he stepped into the room, he caught sight of the food still spread on the table.

"Oh," he said quietly. "You have eaten, I see."

I was surprised to hear myself say, "Maybe you would like to taste some Christmas food?" By then my husband and children had joined us in the kitchen. None of them asked for an explanation of the stranger's presence. I had let him in and that was enough for them. The blond man smiled at them and shook their hands, still calm and trusting as a kitten.

Then he turned to the wood fire range and rubbed his hands together to warm them, glancing over at the dinner table while he stood there. "Yes," he said, in answer to my question. "If you have enough food, it would be very nice."

I relit the candles while the stranger walked around the table looking into the bowls and pots. He seemed unfamiliar with most of the dishes, and when he came to the red cabbage, he stopped and his eyes grew wide.

"But what is this?" he exclaimed. "It is quite black! Is there *blood* in it?"

"No," I assured him. "Red cabbage always turns black when you cook it in an iron pot."

"How strange," he muttered. "Perhaps I won't eat it."

Ham and bread, green cabbage and Christmas sausage, spareribs and peas, he tasted everything slowly and with a look of great concentration.

My little daughter stood close to me, staring quietly while he ate. At last our Christmas guest got up, thanking me for the feast. "If I may borrow the newspaper, I would like to check on the television programs." He got it and started reading while my daughter's eyes followed him, round and thoughtful. "Let's see, how about this show here?"

I looked over his shoulder at the TV guide. "It is too late for that one; was that the one you wanted to see?"

"I do not know," he said. "But this one, look! I am sure that this one is good. I would very much like to see it." He stepped into the little room where our television stood, pulled a chair from near the wall, and planted himself in front of the set. "Now then," he said. "How do you switch this on?"

His words sounded a bit solemn and his strange blue eyes were as eager as a child's, a child expecting a glorious treat.

We switched the set on for him and the whole family sat down to join him. A comedy was just starting, a funny story of the kind that the whole family can watch, even very young children. The stranger did not look at us while the television was on. He followed the story closely, and when the action grew frantic, he threw his head back and laughed so that his angel's hair flew around him.

The film had a happy ending. My husband reached over and snapped off the set. The night was silent outside the house. The stranger was still laughing quietly to himself. "Just imagine," he said softly. "Today I have even laughed."

He turned in his chair and looked at us, still with laughter in his cheeks. He looked carefully at each one of us as if he wanted to remember our faces. We all sat silently for a few minutes.

"Where are you going?" my husband asked.

"To Copenhagen," was his answer. "I come from the north of Sweden and I am going there to save people. There is so much sin there and the people need help."

"How do you travel?" my husband asked again. "By car?"

"No. I walk."

Had he walked the 700 or 800 miles from the north of Sweden to our house in the woods? And was he planning to walk the hundreds of miles south to Denmark as well?

The words hung in the air. The stranger smiled and laughed once again with his strange and carefree tone. "Sometimes kind people give me a ride, sometimes I walk, sometimes I get food, and tonight I have even laughed." His blue eyes twinkled in genuine joy as if he had been given a grand gift.

He and my husband went on talking about this and that for a little while as I sat wondering what to do with our strange guest.

Our daughter pulled at my skirt and whispered, "Mum, is he going to spend the night here?"

I shook my head, quite at a loss. It was the stranger himself who solved the problem. Suddenly he got up and announced that he really must be going.

"Are you really going to…walk?" I asked. "There are no people on the roads tonight and the next town is far away."

"I'll be fine," he said, calmly.

He had this strange smile. It was not polite, not embarrassed. It broke out spontaneously as if he could not hold it back, an eager smile. It seemed as if he were looking forward to something we did not know or as if he had seen something we could not see.

Without thinking, I took a big orange from the fruit bowl and handed it to him. "Here, at least you will have something to eat while you are walking."

His smile broke out again. He took the orange and held it in his hand like a king holding his orb. "Imagine," he said reverently. "This orange has traveled all the way around the world to Sweden and now I am holding it in my hand. Is that not fantastic?"

Suddenly we all saw the orange with his eyes—a fantastic ripe orange from a warm country far, far away—and we too marveled at the sight.

He put the orange into his pocket. His hands were warm when he shook ours.

The Christmas night was absolutely still, cold and clear. The moonlight poured down over the sparkling whiteness and the lonely stranger, who took big steps in the deep snow. His footprints looked like black holes and his shining blond hair was the last we saw of him as he disappeared between the trees on his way back to the main road.

We watched him quietly, and then turned to go back into our warm house. It was my daughter who spoke first.

"Was that Jesus?" she asked.

I smiled an adult's smile. "No, it was not. You know, it is a very long time since Jesus was born on Christmas."

"I know!" she said impatiently. "But he can come whenever he wants to, can't he? I think that was Jesus!"

The next morning, on Christmas Day, we tried to follow the stranger's deep footprints toward the main road. But suddenly, we had to stop. Right there, in the middle of our own little path out to the road, the footprints suddenly ceased. We looked all around us at the pure untouched snow. No footprints, no car tire marks, absolutely nothing.

When we came to know our neighbors in the following months we always asked if they had seen a stranger walking alone on the road that Christmas night. No one had seen any sign of a stranger.

We never learned who the stranger was, or how he disappeared. But we cannot help wondering....

—KERSTIN BACKMAN
Grängesberg, Sweden

O Christmas Tree

HRISTMAS 1990 FOUND OUR FAMILY in a new home in California, due to my husband's job transfer. We missed the beautiful snow-covered mountains of our Utah home; the weepy drizzle and fog of our new location felt strange and depressing during the holiday season. We longed for the traditions of a white Christmas complete with sledding, snowmen in our front yard, and playful snowball fights with our four young daughters. Cozy holiday get-togethers with Grandma, aunts, uncles, and cousins were now replaced with cordial neighborhood parties given by well-meaning but nevertheless unfamiliar new acquaintances. But we were determined to "bloom where we were planted" and we tried to remain cheerful in spite of feeling dreadfully homesick.

We had hoped to make the six-hundred-mile trek back to see our families sometime during the holiday, but the economy had taken a nose-dive that year and our budget wouldn't allow any unnecessary extravagance. At least we had a nice new home, which was cheerfully decked from floor to ceiling with ornaments, ribbons, boughs, and lights we had collected over the years. And then there was our tree. It stood in the big bay window of our living room and was covered with all the beautiful glass ornaments I had so carefully wrapped months before, not wanting to lose a single one during our move. Our house was located on the corner of a well-traveled street and I knew the tree looked radiant to all those who drove by.

The evening of December 12 our girls were begging to sleep under the tree in their sleeping bags as we often did as a family, reading Christmas stories and munching on goodies. Although I had sometimes allowed this tradition even on school nights in December, my practical side took over and I reminded them that there would be plenty of nights for this after school closed for the holidays. A little disgruntled and teasing me that I had turned into a "Scrooge," they finally settled down for the night, two girls in each bedroom.

About 2:00 A.M. we were suddenly shocked out of our sleep by a loud crash followed instantly by the deafening scream of our burglar alarm. My husband, Greg, leaped from our bed and, being a Vietnam vet, instinctively grabbed his gun, yelling at me to call 911. Knowing I wouldn't be able to communicate over the shriek of the alarm, I punched in the code numbers to turn it off. Then I called for help. When the 911 operator asked the nature of the emergency, I hysterically responded that I didn't know except that our house had been broken into, setting off our alarm. Almost at the same moment, I heard Greg yelling that our house had been hit by a car! The operator asked for our address. Firemen were on their way. We invited a very drunk driver into our house to call his parents, and he was taken away in handcuffs by the police moments later. Neighbors gathered in pajamas and robes, shaking their heads in disbelief and offering words of comfort. A capable crew of public servants worked for hours to clean up the debris, scooping our treasures like trash out into the yard. Plastic sheets were put up in an effort to contain our house and protect it from the elements for the few remaining hours before daylight.

Morning came and, yes, our nightmare was a reality. Assessing the damage in the light of day was shocking: The car had come right through our bay window and knocked down the whole front wall along with the window. Of course, our tree, along with many other precious possessions, was demolished. As we scrounged through the heaps of trash, looking for anything to salvage, we noticed a houseplant that had been across the room from the Christmas tree, with a perfect round hole in one of its large leaves. On closer examination, we discovered a small round ornament sitting unbroken in the dirt. The ornament had shot through the leaf with such violent force that it had punched a hole through the leaf in its exact shape. Although we had lost many beautiful things in the accident, we were suddenly aware of the deadly impact of the crash, and were humbly grateful that our four little blond girls had not been sleeping under the tree, as they had so desperately wanted to do the night before. As their mother, I knew in my heart I had been prompted to be uncompromising in my insistence that they sleep in their own rooms that night. We were heartsick over our losses, but we were becoming vaguely aware of the miracles that were just beginning.

As the details of the night unfolded, we learned that our girls had acted heroically. In one room, our daughter Gretchen had instructed her younger sister to hurry into the closet. In the other bedroom, Lauryn had told her younger sister to get under the bed. Even in their own terror, their thoughts were for each other's safety. The emotional damage, however, took longer to heal than the physical damage. It would be weeks before the girls would feel secure in their own beds. They, too, realized how easily someone could have been seriously injured.

Driving through our neighborhood that morning, a building contractor named Steve Larsen noticed the mess and, wondering how a tornado had struck only one house on the block, stopped to offer his help. He became our dear friend over the next few weeks and was able to work miracles in getting our house repaired in fairly short order. Considering how slowly the gears of the legal system turned, and our complicated insurance policies, this process could have taken months to get going, but Steve's compassionate efforts resulted in the rebuilding beginning that very day. He was even able to acquire a new bay window for us from a manufacturer who had a month-long waiting list. I remember one of his subcontractors confiding in us that, although he was very sorry for our situation, he was also thankful for the work. He hadn't worked for many months and this job meant that his family would be able to have a Christmas.

Our phone rang constantly with offers of help. "Do you need meals brought in while you are trying to clean up?... Are you warm enough?...Do you need heaters?...Should we organize some men from the neighborhood to watch your house until it is secure so you can sleep at night?" Neighbors who previously had given only a nod or an obligatory wave now stopped to introduce themselves, expressing their concern and leaving their phone numbers in case we needed anything. Unfamiliar joggers and walkers who had previously seen happy girls playing in the front yard now stopped to inquire about our daughters, expressing relief that no one had been injured or killed. We began to feel the arms of love that would hold us up over the next several months.

The night of the church Christmas party was fast approaching, and although Greg and I certainly weren't in a partying mood and were exhausted from all the cleanup, we decided that the girls needed to attend something normal and festive during the holidays. When everyone at the party started singing carols, I choked back tears, feeling like I couldn't remain cheerful or positive one more minute, in light of the incredibly stressful week we had just experienced. When the evening was finally over, we came home, glad to roll our tired bodies into bed for a few precious hours of sleep. Just at that moment, we suddenly heard people singing outside—carolers on the front porch. My heart sank. I just knew I couldn't force one more smile for a group of jubilant people, much less open the door to reveal my disheveled house.

But it was too late. One of the girls quickly opened the door and we stood there in our pajamas, listening to thirty or forty familiar voices sing "O Christmas

Tree, O Christmas Tree, how lovely *were* your branches!" The song continued with words specially created for our circumstances, from friends with eyes full of caring and love. I don't remember the words to the song as much as I remember our feelings, as small wrapped packages started being passed over the heads of the carolers and into our arms. We each took several in our hands and had to put them down to receive the rest. We were instructed to "open *before* Christmas" and then the group excused themselves, as the hour was late.

We stared in wonder at the pile of gifts. As we gathered in a circle and began to unwrap each one, our hearts were full as we saw before us scores of new ornaments for a future tree: beautiful glass icicles, angels, a blown-glass heart, a bit of felt on which "JOY" had been stitched in sequins, a delicate silver nativity. One creative couple with a sense of humor had hammered a matchbox car and attached a hook to it; it took its rightful place among the more elegant ornaments. Handmade, store-bought, each ornament was a token of love and an effort to "bear ye one another's burdens…" (Gal. 6:2). New priceless treasures from new cherished friends. We were indeed loved.

Christmas 1996 found the Gardner family somewhat melancholy as we watched the drippy drizzle from the Utah skies. Another job transfer had replanted us back in our beautiful snow-covered mountains, and although we were happy to be with old friends and family, we longed for our California friends. For, in five short years, through good times and bad, we had grown to love another "family" in a place we could truly call "home."

—JANNIS GARDNER
Sandy, Utah

Chester

HESTER FIRST CAME INTO OUR FAMILY with a tough assignment: win over five people who didn't want him. He had the unenviable task of replacing Coots, our lovable tiger cat, who had just died of feline leukemia. My father, brother, two younger sisters, and I were so heartbroken over the loss of Coots that we decided it was best not to have a pet for a while—so we were all shocked the early December afternoon when my mother came home with a tiny black-and-white fur ball with pink paws in her arms.

Chester Festus Aldo Emery was the name we eventually settled on, and he took the job of winning us over very seriously. By Christmas, after he'd only been with us a few weeks and was still tiny and fragile, he would sneak out of his bed in the middle of the night, scale the stairs, nestle himself on my pillow, and purr contentedly.

As the months and years passed, Chester's unique quirks continually endeared him to me—quirks such as walking around the rim of the bathtub whenever I took a bath, hiding in empty paper bags, hopping onto the Lazy Susan whenever it was opened, and wanting to perch himself on my shoulders when I walked through the house. But the most peculiar thing about him was his love for playing fetch with a minature nylon flag. The ratty, hole-filled white flag with the blue words FAIRBANKS MUSEUM was stapled to a small black stick. At precisely six-thirty every night, as I sat doing homework or watching TV,

Chester would enter my room with the flag between his teeth and drop it at my feet. I'd throw it down the stairs, and like a dog he'd bound after it. I'd hear the quick patter of his paws going down, then up, and within seconds he'd be back, whiskers twitching, tail wagging, puffing like a race car and raring to do it again. This would go on for about twenty-five throws per session or until I'd finally had enough—he could have gone on indefinitely.

Chester was a house cat, and never seemed interested in going outdoors, but sometimes he lingered just a little too close to the door for my liking. Whenever someone knocked on the door, or the door was opened, the refrain "Make sure the cat doesn't get out!" could be heard through the house, and it was me doing the talking. Just to make sure, I'd usually rush to the door to be certain that Chester was safe.

The day after Thanksgiving, during my senior year in high school, I had just thrown the flag down the stairs for the first time that night when I heard a light tap at the front door. Before I had a chance to look down the stairwell, the door had been opened. It was our neighbor, Charlie Williams, a close friend of the family who was in the habit of opening the door before we could get to it. Charlie's heavy boot entered the hall and landed squarely on Chester's tail. A high-pitched yowl followed and before my foot hit the top stair, Chester was out the door.

We finally quit searching after three hours. Calling his name in the darkness did no good. There was no sign of the flag, no sign of anything. In three years, Chester had never been out, and his survival prospects weren't that good—especially with a Doberman and a German shepherd in the neighborhood, both of which ran free, and the fact that we lived at the corner of the busiest traffic intersection in town.

I was up before dawn, out looking again. Nothing. No traces, which was good, I figured; at least he wasn't in the road. I went door to door in the neighborhood; we posted signs, called the radio station, took out newspaper ads, everything. Nothing at all materialized. It was as though Chester had vanished into thin air. I went out onto the front porch every night calling his name while my brother and sisters cried behind me.

As the days passed, it was hard to get through a day of school without the tears welling up, especially after ten inches of snow fell. Winter was settling in to northeast Vermont, and with it the grim reality that I'd never see Chester again.

I had trouble sleeping at night because I missed his warm circle on my pillow and his licking my face in the morning. Finally, a few days before Christmas, my parents told me I should stop calling for Chester because it was bothering the other kids too much.

On a very sad Christmas Eve, as we were getting ready to go to bed, we got a frantic call from our neighbor Charlie, the friend who had accidentally let Chester out that night in November. A water pipe had burst in his basement and he needed help fixing it. My father, an excellent handyman, got some tools together and he and I headed over to help out next door.

Charlie's cellar was a mess. Water was spraying in all directions, soaking piles of laundry, wood, family mementos, everything. "Thank goodness we didn't hide the children's Christmas presents down here!" Charlie said, as he surveyed the chaos. My father soon found the source of the leak and we began to patch it up. After about half an hour it was repaired well enough to hold for a few days. From the stairwell, we looked around the basement one more time.

In a far corner, sticking out from behind a covered woodpile, a soiled, white piece of nylon caught my eye. "Wait a minute, Dad!" I said, and I moved toward it, slowly at first, and then very quickly. In the faint light I reached down and picked it up. My eyes flooded with tears when I realized it was Chester's flag. I crouched down and shone my flashlight into the crack behind the pile. Two feet in, looking back at me, were two cloudy, barely open cat eyes in a head that no longer had the strength to move. I yelled out and both Charlie and my father rushed back down the stairs. We carefully moved the wood off the pile to get to Chester.

"He must have fallen through the cellar window and been too scared to meow," Charlie said. "He's probably been down here the whole month. I covered the cellar windows with plastic on the last Saturday in November."

Frail and thin, Chester wasn't far from death. I gently picked him up. His eyes closed with relief. He was breathing, but just barely. As I carried him up the stairs, I placed the flag on his stomach and could hear the faint sound of purring and feel the muscles in his tail futilely attempting to wag.

Miraculously, after a visit to the vet and several weeks of tender loving care, Chester pulled through and returned to his old sprightly self. He lived with our family for many happy years after that. What might have been one of our saddest family holidays became instead one of our most memorable, and now, almost fifteen years later, I still place that tattered old flag on the Christmas tree every year in honor of Chester.

—JOHN EMERY
Clifton Park, New York

One Last Wish

UR CHRISTMAS MIRACLE started early that year—in January, to be exact. That was symbolic in many ways. The first of the year—a new beginning—a starting-over place. Expectations, hopes, dreams, and goals. A perfect time for miracles.

I've heard it said that there are no small miracles. And ours would not be small. We would learn important lessons of life that would change us in ways still hard for us to comprehend. We had struggled through so many losses the previous year. The loss of our family business, personal finances, our family home, and more important, our dreams. Yes, that year left us humble and meager, but the struggle made us stronger and wiser.

We were excited to start a new year. Never had we possessed so little and believed so much. Nineteen ninety-four—that was to be our year. A year of rebuilding, healing, and recovery. However, nothing we dreamed of or planned could have prepared us for the events that would soon take place.

It was cold and dark on that special night in January when my husband, Cal, first heard it. We had just started a new business and Cal was working alone in one of his back offices. He suddenly heard the voice of a small girl calling out, "Daddy...Daddy...Daddy." Thinking that a little girl had gotten lost, he searched the outside reception area, and even the parking lot. Finding no one, he returned to his office to finish his work. Then he heard the girl's voice again: "Daddy...Daddy...Daddy." Because he was alone in the office, Cal tried to come up with a logical explanation. When he came home that night, he told me about his experience. He seemed bewildered, and yet neither of us could find any answers, and so with a family to care for, we turned our attention to other responsibilities.

It was only a few days later on a peaceful, quiet afternoon at home when she came. Cal was watching a sporting event on television downstairs; I was upstairs trying to catch up on a project. I suddenly heard the sound of Cal's footsteps running up the stairs and I could hear the heaviness of his breath even before he found me. White as a sheet and shaking, he reached our for me. His words tumbled over each other in his haste to tell me what had happened. He had been sitting in his chair watching the game on TV when he heard again the voice of a small girl calling out. It was a clear voice, very close and soft. "Daddy, Daddy, Daddy." Cal quickly turned his head toward the voice and saw a small girl standing just a few feet away from his chair, looking directly into his eyes. He jumped out of the chair and turned again to find her gone. Then he ran up the stairs to find me.

Now this was something we couldn't explain away or simply dismiss from our minds. What could it mean? Why had this happened? Was God trying to tell us something, and if so, what? Could this be our child? It didn't make any sense. We had a total of eight children between us: four of them married, a daughter at college, and three boys at home. After having three boys in a row, could this be the daughter I had dreamed of and longed for? But why now, so late in our lives? I couldn't fathom it and jokingly replied, "Honey, maybe she meant to say 'Grandpa,' but it was too big a word for such a little girl." Yet as I prayed that night, I asked for answers: Was a daughter to come to our family? At our age? With eight other children? What of our finances, or lack of them? And then, as I had become accustomed to doing, I concluded with a simple "Thy will be done."

It came as no surprise when, a few weeks later, I found I was carrying a baby. Knowing it was to be a girl, I rushed to the fabric store and came home with arms full of pink fabric. I sewed blankets, dresses, comforters, and crib sets, all in pink! I sewed my way through the summer and into fall. Cal was working hard to develop his clientele for his new business in addition to working as a sales manager for a dealership. By November, he was feeling exhausted and I was very overdue. But as if the year had not produced enough incredible experiences already, we were in for yet another surprise.

Cal had been saying he had a stomachache for a few weeks. Because he rarely complained, although he had experienced pain most of his life due to a birth defect, I was concerned. I thought perhaps he had an ulcer from all the stress of the past two years, and so he went in for some routine tests. Shortly after he returned from having some X rays taken, his doctor called us at home. "Mrs. Stewart," she said, "I need to see you and your husband in my office in one hour." I was immediately overcome with a feeling of despair.

The air in the doctor's office was thick and heavy. I was very uncomfortable, being twenty-one days overdue, and Cal struggled quietly with his own pain. The doctor's words came quickly and were straight to the point: "Mr. and Mrs. Stewart, I am sorry to tell you that Cal has cancer. It seems to have started in your esophagus, but it has spread to your liver, stomach, and lymph nodes. It is terminal. I hope you will live to see the birth of your child."

For a minute I thought I was losing my mind. I could hardly believe I had heard the doctor say she hoped Cal would live to see the birth of his child. Couldn't she see I was due to deliver at any moment? I felt my head spinning as I tried to listen to what she was saying and keep myself from crying. We stumbled from her office to the car. I don't know how we got home. I do remember being at the foot of our bed that afternoon, holding hands as Cal offered up to God the desires of his heart, asking for a healing, a blessing. He cried. I had been with him for so many years, decades almost, and could only remember him crying two times before.

Over the next few days we went from doctor to doctor and tried to make plans. Cal had decided he was not going to die from cancer. Other people had survived such a thing, so why not Cal?

Just three days after his diagnosis, on November 19, our daughter was born. Little Rebecca created quite a stir as she made her entrance into the world that night. What a wonderful event it was! The room was full of family, children, and friends. During the whole ordeal, I felt Cal at my side, his arm around my shoulder and his hand on my arm. My support, my strength, as he had always been. I didn't notice then how sick he had become that day. And it wouldn't be until Christmas that he would tell me about the other touching events of that evening. He said that he had felt fine during the whole night, until the moment Rebecca was born. As he touched her little body as she lay on my chest and as he realized she was all right, he began to feel himself slipping away. He struggled for a chair and quietly fought the feeling of death that had overcome him at the very moment life had entered his newborn baby.

In the wee hours of the morning, Cal, on bended knees, pleaded for his life. Humbly and with faith, he begged for more time. Not for himself—he now knew it was his time to go—but for his children, his wife. How could he leave her on the night she had just given birth? Who would take care of her, or the other children? "Please, please," he begged, "for my wife, my children, please give me more time. Please just give me Christmas."

It was dawn before he struggled up from his knees and fell into bed. God would grant him his last wish.

And so on Christmas we celebrated. We celebrated life, family, the blessings God had given us. We celebrated the birth of His Son, Jesus Christ, and the birth of our perfect little daughter. Family and friends came from across the country to be with us on Cal's last Christmas. It was a joyous time as we felt the love of so many around us.

And then Christmas was over—the carolers were gone from our doorstep, family and friends returned to their homes, the tree and the lights were taken down, and Cal's body ceased to struggle against the disease.

We slept with him in the hospital those last nights—Rebecca and I on a cot by his bed; another daughter, Rachel, in a chair. The cancer had spread to his brain, and he no longer could talk or see, or even stay awake. But for two days I watched in awe as another miracle unfolded. As each of his eight children came to say good-bye to their father—their hero—Cal would wake up, sit up in his bed, and listen to each child, and then share his love and tender feelings with each one.

The last day we were alone together. I crawled up into the hospital bed with him and tried to express the feelings of my heart. I felt so helpless without him—he had always taken care of me, of all of us. I talked to him for hours, reminding him of all the love and laughter we had shared, the dreams, the wonderful experiences of our life together. I thanked him for teaching me by his great example to love, to trust, to give. I thanked him for each of our beautiful children, for his strength, his patience, his forgiving heart. And I thanked him for waiting—for enduring his own pain to give us that last wonderful Christmas together.

And then I let him go. I assured him that the children and I would be all right. He could go now to his heavenly home.

The little girl who had come to visit her "Daddy" almost a year before would now be the angel that would hold our family together through our extraordinary grief. Day by day, little Rebecca brought such joy and love to our broken hearts that we were able to begin healing. Cal had not only lasted through Christmas; he had given our family the greatest of all gifts—a part of himself that would last a lifetime.

—CYNTHIA STEWART-COPIER
Roseville, California

In memory of Calvin Eugene Stewart.

Bologna from Heaven

 Y GRANDMOTHER WAS NOT the "homebaked cookies and crocheted blankies grandma" sort at all.

She had lived the majority of her life as a widow with two children, working hard as a professional in a world unaccustomed to such things. A southern lady of appreciable means, she had hired help when my mother and my aunt were being raised, giving her distance from the day-to-day chores of child rearing. She was formal, aloof, almost Victorian—and utterly undomestic. From my earliest days I called her "Grandmother," so that you could practically hear the capital "G."

She certainly didn't know what to do with her first grandchild, a girl, who came to Winder, Georgia, for week-long summer visits. Grandmother's life was utterly adult, from the hard-edged brocade furniture and untouchable baby grand piano in her living room to her habit of living in solitary peace, eating most meals out. The presence of grandchildren had a way of complicating the routine.

Breakfast was easy enough: cereal. And we could always go out for dinner. But lunch was trickier—while she often skipped it herself, this was not an option for a growing young child. For the brief duration of those summer visits, she did the best she could to overcome her lack of culinary interest and skill.

Fried bologna sandwiches were the answer. At noontime while she cooked, I would sit on the white enameled table next to the stove, its smooth surface cool under my summertanned legs, my feet dangling off the edge. The slap of distant screen doors slamming and the squeals of neighbors' grandchildren playing in the midday heat poured in through the open window behind me.

I loved the ritual of preparing the sandwiches as much as the food itself. My job was to carefully peel away the red rubbery shell from each piece of bologna. Grandmother would put it into a hot, heavy cast-iron skillet, cooking only one slice at a time. I watched intently for the best part to happen—when heat made the bologna puff up in the center to resemble a pink bathing cap, with great force Grandmother would deflate the little cap with two businesslike whacks with the edge of a metal spatula, making a little cross in the center of the slice. Soon after that special step, the bologna was flipped over, and when the edges began to curl up from the heat, it was done. Placed on toasted white bread liberally slathered with Hellmann's mayonnaise, it was my lunch every day in Winder, Georgia.

As an adult I rarely eat meat at all, much less a highly processed product of such questionable origin and ingredients as bologna. The sylvan days of hot Georgia summers are a long time away from my life today.

Grandmother had died the year I was married. Soon divorced, in dire financial straits from my former husband's shenanigans, and estranged from the rest of my family, I found myself living in a small, low-budget apartment shared with a roommate. Struggling to finish my college education on small student loans and slow-to-arrive grants, I was faced with a poor and lonely Christmas.

The contrast between my own plain life and the artificial gaiety that decorated the town was depressing. Christmas lights and silver tinsel hung from lampposts; huge winking stars decorated the intersections. My apartment was not decorated at all—I had no Christmas tree, no honey-baked ham, no tin of home-baked cookies on my table. The only bright spot in my life that year was my two little Pekingese dogs, Sandy and Samantha. They loved me unconditionally and were a tremendous source of comfort during those rough years.

Alas, not only did I have no tree, no ham, and no cookies, but I also had no dog food. No dog food and no money in my checking account. My next student loan payment was not scheduled to arrive for another week or so, and as the nursery rhyme says, my cupboards were bare. Now I could have made it for a week on my own without food, casually dropping in on friends near dinnertime or swallowing my pride and visiting a soup kitchen for a hot meal. But how could I feed my "girls"? Studying the figures in my checkbook, unable to find a forgotten dollar or a calculating mistake, I realized that the only way I could feed my little family was to write a check at the store while knowing full well that it would not be covered until my student loan arrived. I was horrified that this was the level to which I had sunk, sick at heart to think that I was about to resort to a life of crime, and depressed that there was no one to whom I could turn, no one to comfort me.

I screwed up my resolve and decided to "buy" only the most minimal essentials, not wanting to take advantage of the grocery store any more than I had to. No steak or lobster for me, just the basics. I wrote grocery list after grocery list, paring the items down to where I had but a few things that the dogs and I could not do without.

It was a long car ride to the local market. I entered with a heavy heart and slowly walked the aisles to find the few things on my list. Dog food, bread, milk, Top Ramen. Standing in line at the checkout counter, I was certain that everyone around me could sense what I was about to do. Christmas carols played over the sound system as I fidgeted. Finally it was my turn at the register. Blinking through tears of shame, I wrote out the check and handed it to the checkout girl. "Thank you. Have a merry Christmas," she said. I grabbed my bag and ran for the car.

I wept the whole way back to the apartment. What was my life coming to? Would I ever finish school, and would I ever get back on track financially?

Once home and unpacking my plunder, I reached into the sack for the last few items when my hand found an unfamiliar plastic package, cool to the touch. Puzzled, I pulled it out.

It was a five-pound package of Oscar Meyer bologna.

Bologna? That wasn't on my list! I hadn't eaten it in years, and I knew full well I hadn't put it into my cart at the store; it was way too expensive for me to "afford." I checked the receipt—the bologna wasn't there.

And then it hit me. Grandmother. She was trying to take care of me. From across the heavens she'd felt my hunger, my fear, and my despair, and she had reached out through the mists to comfort and care for me the only way she'd ever known how—with fried bologna sandwiches. Hours before, I'd been at the brink of starvation; now I had enough bologna and bread to eat until the next check arrived.

Crying again but this time from joy, I reached for a frying pan and set about making the best Christmas dinner I'd ever had. Every year since then I make fried bologna sandwiches on Christmas Eve, thwacking the puffed-up slices with the side of my spatula and remembering an extraordinary woman from Winder, Georgia.

—Nora Lynn
Sacramento, California

The Town That Gave Christmas

T WAS CHRISTMAS EVE, 1927, in the remote prairie town of
Hillspring, Alberta, Canada. Mary Thomas Jeppson was getting her
six small children ready for bed. She thought her heart would break
as she watched five of her children dance around the small house,
excited to hang their socks for Santa to fill. Her oldest daughter, Ellen, sat
subdued and sullen in a corner of the cold, two-room house. Ellen's heart was
heavy for a ten-year-old, but she understood the reality of what tomorrow would
bring. She felt that her mother was cruel to let the children get their hopes up
when she knew very well there would be nothing to fill the socks. They would
be lucky to have a little mush for breakfast, as there was only a small amount of
wheat and corn left. The winter had just started and already it was cold and
harsh. The milk cow had died the week before from starvation and severe
weather conditions, and the last two or three chickens had stopped laying eggs
about a month before.

Mary helped each one of the children hang a little darned and mended sock.
She tried to persuade Ellen to hang one, too, but Ellen just sat there, shaking
her head and mumbling "Mom, don't do this. Don't pretend." After the socks
had been hung, Mary read the Christmas story from the Bible and then recited a

few Christmas poems from memory—and memories of her own happy childhood living in the United States flooded her mind. She was the next to youngest of a very large and loving family. Although they'd been pioneers in a remote area of Idaho, her mother and father had made life—and especially Christmas—very exciting and memorable.

Before Ellen went to bed, she pleaded with her mother to tell the children the truth. Mary kissed her daughter good night and whispered, "I can't, Ellen. Don't ask me why—I just can't tell them." It was almost midnight and the other children had been asleep for hours, and Mary's husband Leland had gone to bed, too, feeling like a broken man, like he had failed his family completely. Mary sat by the fire reading the Christmas story from the Bible over and over again. Her mind drifted to her plight here in this godforsaken land of ice and snow. It was the beginning of the Depression and her husband had heard wondrous stories about the unlimited opportunities of homesteading in Canada. After two years of not being able to find work in the United States and after a flood had destroyed their small home in Willard, Utah, he had decided to move his family to Canada. It seemed, however, that they were five or six years too late to cash in on the rumored opportunities. After several seasons of unusual weather conditions, most of their crops had frozen or failed.

In October Mary had received a letter from her family back in Idaho, asking what they could do to help and what they could send the family for Christmas. Mary had put off her response—she had too much pride to let them know how destitute her family really was. Finally in November, realizing that things were not going to get any better, she had written. She only mentioned the necessities: She told them how desperately they needed food, especially wheat, yeast, flour, and cornmeal. She related how long it had been since she had been able to bake a cake or cookies, because they had no molasses or honey, and of course, no sugar. It had been a year since they had had any salt to use on their food. She also added that it would be wonderful if they could ship just a little bit of coal, because of the cold, and because their fuel supply was almost depleted. She finished her letter with a request for some old, used quilts. All of hers had worn thin and were full of holes, and it was difficult keeping the children warm. She mentioned their need for anything to keep them warm— any used socks, shoes or gloves, warm hats or coats. And at the very end of the letter she wrote, "If you could just find a dress that someone has outgrown that I could make over to fit Ellen, please send that, too. Ellen is such a little old lady for such a young girl. She carries the worries of the whole family on her thin shoulders. She has only one dress that she wears all the time, and it is patched and faded. She has outgrown it, and I would like so very much to fix up something that is nicer for her."

The week before Christmas, Leland hitched up the horse and sleigh and made the three-hour round trip from Hillspring into the town of Cardston every day to check at the train station and post office whether a package had come from their family in Idaho. Each day, he received the same disappointing answer. Finally, on the day before Christmas, he went into Cardston first thing in the morning and eagerly waited for the mail delivery. He left in the early afternoon to get home before dark and he left empty-handed. He wept openly as he rode home, knowing he would have to explain to Mary that perhaps the package would arrive the day after Christmas or the next week, but that it had not made it in time for the big day.

Mary suddenly awoke from her reminiscent sleep with a chill. The old clock on the wall said it was 3:30 A.M. The fire in the stove was all but out and she decided to add a little more fuel so that it wouldn't take so long to start in the morning. She looked over at the little limp socks still hanging by the fireplace and felt a similar emptiness in her heart. Outside, the wind was blowing at about seventy miles per hour—the snowstorm had intensified. Mary was about to put out the lantern and go to bed for a few short hours, when she heard a quiet knock at the door. Mary opened the door to find a man standing there, and in all her life she had never seen anyone look more like her vision of Santa Claus. He was covered with ice and snow and had a long beard, made white from the snow. His hat, his gloves, and boots were also white, and for a moment Mary thought she was dreaming.

It was the mailman, Mr. Scow from Cardston, who had known the plight of the Jeppson family. He told her that he knew they had been waiting for packages from Idaho and he knew there would be no Christmas without them. That evening, as he was finishing up a long day of delivering mail all around the town, he was glad to be going home. His horse was exhausted and frozen as that day there had been one of the worst blizzards of the year. He was relieved to put his horse in the barn, park his sleigh, and return to the warmth of Christmas Eve at home with his family. But just as he was leaving, someone from the train station came running up to him and told him that ten large crates had just arrived from the States for the Jeppson family. It was only about four in the afternoon, but already it was dark and the storm was getting worse. They both decided there was nothing they could do about delivering the crates that night, but that they would be sure the Jeppsons received them the day after Christmas.

The mailman told Mary that when he went home, he had a disturbing feeling, and after discussing it with his wife, they decided that he needed to deliver the crates that night. He would have to find someone who would let him borrow a fresh horse and a sleigh with sharp running blades. After he finished telling Mary about his decision to come, he brought the crates into the house. She insisted that he thaw out and warm up by the stove while she went out to check on his horse. When she looked at the poor animal with icicles hanging from its nose and mouth, she knew it would never make the trip back to Cardston that night and she tried to talk Mr. Scow into staying until morning.

He refused the offer, telling her that it had taken him almost eight hours to make the trip to her house in the storm, and if he were to leave now, he would still be able to spend Christmas afternoon with his family. So Mary told him she would harness their own horse, which was in better condition, to make the trip back. She got him some dry clothes, fed him what warm food she could muster, and he headed off to town. It was almost 5:00 A.M. and he probably wouldn't get home until around noon. Mary had thanked him as best she could, but for her whole life she maintained that there would never be sufficient words to express her gratitude. "After all," she would say, "how do you thank someone for a miracle...and a Christmas miracle at that?"

As soon as he left, Mary began to unpack the crates. She a only had an hour or so before the children would awaken. At the top of one of the crates she found a letter from her sisters. As she began to read the incredible account, tears streamed down her face. They told her that quilting bees had been held all over the Malad Valley, and from these, six thick, warm, beautiful quilts were included. They told her of the many women who had sewn shirts for the boys and dresses for the girls, and of others who had knitted the warm gloves and hats. The donation of socks and shoes had come from people from miles around. The local church had even held a bazaar to raise the money to buy new coats and scarves for the whole family. All of the sisters, nieces and cousins, aunts and uncles had gathered to bake the breads and make the candy. There was even a crate half full of beef that had been cured and packed so that it could be shipped, along with two or three slabs of bacon and two hams. At the close of the letter, her sisters said, "We hope you have a merry Christmas, and thank you so much for making our Christmas the best one we've ever had!"

When Mary's family awoke that Christmas morning, they did so to the sound of bacon sizzling on the stove and the smell of hot cinnamon muffins coming from the little oven. There were bottles of syrup and jars of jam, and canned fruit, including kinds that the younger children had never even seen before. Every sock that was hanging was stuffed with homemade taffy, fudge, divinity, and dried fruit of every kind. The children didn't even know the names of some of the cookies and goodies that lay before them. Later Mary and Leland were to find tucked in each toe of the stockings that had been sent for them, a few dollars and a note stating that the money was to be used to buy coal and fuel for the rest of the winter, and oats and wheat to feed the animals.

For each boy there was a bag of marbles, and each girl had a little rag doll made just for her. But the most wonderful moment of the whole day was when Ellen awoke, the last to get up, and walked over to the spot where she had refused to hang her sock the night before. She rubbed her eyes in disbelief as she saw hanging there a beautiful red Christmas dress, trimmed with white and green satin ribbons. Ellen turned around, walked back to her bed, and lay down, thinking she was dreaming. After her little sisters pounced on her with laughter and excitement, she came back again to the celebration and joy of the most wonderful Christmas ever. For that morning, along with the aroma of good food, the love of a good family, and a new red dress, a childhood had been given back to a young girl—a childhood of hopes and dreams, of Santa Claus, and of the wonder of Christmas.

I will never forget the retelling of this story by my mother, Mary Thomas Jeppson. Although it was always an emotional drain for her, it was an inspiration to all those who were privileged to hear her story every Christmas since that magical day in 1927.

—MARIAN JEPPSON WALKER
South Jordan, Utah

Merry Christmas,
Mrs. Moring

ANNY MORING HAD SETTLED DOWN to watch the eleven o'clock news in the den of his quiet home in Charleston, South Carolina. His children were tucked in bed. His wife, Allyson, who had complained of a bad case of the flu, was asleep at the other end of the house. Her illness was so severe—fever, chills, cramps, vomiting—that she had isolated herself so she would not pass along the bug to the rest of the family.

Suddenly Danny heard an odd scuffling noise in the kitchen. He went to look. There lay Allyson, curled on the floor in a fetal position. She had pulled herself all the way from their bedroom and now reached toward him, her face distorted in pain. "Danny, help me. I'm dying," she gasped, her teeth chartering. "I really am."

Her husband was stunned. Allyson, thirty-six, had enjoyed wonderful health—except recent surgery for a ruptured spinal disk. Only the day before, she, Danny, and their children—Elizabeth, nine, and Robert, one—had returned home from a Thanksgiving weekend camping trip.

Danny looked down at Allyson; the skin on her fingers and toes was turning purple. He carried her back to their bedroom and called 911. Then he stroked the wet, dark hair plastered to her face and hugged her icy body to him. Minutes later, when the emergency crew arrived, Allyson's blood pressure was undetectable. She was placed on a gurney and carried from the house. Standing in the doorway as the ambulance sped off into the night, Danny felt weak. Of all people, how could this be happening to Allyson? Danny phoned his father to come stay with the children, who were sound asleep. In his mind he could see them, snuggled in bed, innocent to the fact that the very heart of their lives had been plucked out and taken away.

For years now, with her high spirits and smiling slate-blue eyes, Mrs. Moring had won over the hearts of the fifty choral students at Bishop England High School where she taught. They loved to watch her drive into the parking lot, her head bobbing energetically as she filled the car with her own rendition of "I Could Have Danced All Night." Even at her most intense moments of conducting, her face was lit by a half smile.

Since her earliest days, Allyson had loved music. From the age of five, she had taken piano lessons, and later voice lessons. As a teacher, she believed that music could change lives for the better—that it could foster emotional development and enhance all the good aspects of life, the serious as well as the frivolous. She believed, too, that it could soothe those parts of life that are most difficult. In every sense, Allyson Moring was an apostle for the power of music.

For the 1994 Christmas concert, Mrs. Moring's group was attempting one of music's most difficult choral pieces, the "Hallelujah" chorus from Handel's Messiah. A challenge even for adults, the selection would be the centerpiece of the concert—if the students could get it right. For sixteen long weeks, the boys and girls had practiced after school, perfecting simpler selections and struggling with Handel's masterpiece. During Mrs. Moring's absence for back surgery, Katherine Allen, seventeen, a senior who had taken a course in directing music, filled in. But Katherine, slight of build with long blond hair, had found it hard to manage the large group. Believing she had failed as a conductor, she vowed she would stick to singing and leave directing to others.

Allyson Moring returned to choir practice, the success of her surgery marred only by a staph infection, for which she was given antibiotics. She finished the medication on Thanksgiving Saturday. Within hours, she had taken to bed with what she believed to be flu.

When Danny Moring reached the hospital, the news was brutally bad. Medicine's oldest enemy, massive systemic infection, also known as sepsis, had laid siege to his wife's body. She had gone into septic shock, in which bacteria overwhelm the body's systems, blood vessels begin to leak, and vital organs start shutting down. A doctor took Danny aside and suggested he gather the family. There was little chance that Allyson would survive the night.

The next afternoon, the choral group met to talk about Mrs. Moring. The latest medical reports were dire. She had survived the night, but had been given the last rites by the parish priest. It would be almost impossible to stage the Christmas concert, only ten days away. But, more important, what could they do now for Mrs. Moring? One of the students had an idea.

Allyson Moring's infection raged on. At first, in her delirium, she had mumbled about the Christmas concert, telling Danny it had to go on. Then she became totally unresponsive, and was kept alive only by a respirator. Her body swelled so horribly with toxic fluids that her eyes disappeared into bloated flesh.

Danny was standing vigil at her bedside when two of Allyson's colleagues from Bishop England came to the intensive care unit and handed Danny an audiocasserte. "From Allyson's students," they said.

Danny inserted the tape into a small player and turned it on. In a sudden burst, the joyful voices of girls and boys singing Christmas carols filled the cubicle. Staring into Allyson's face, Danny prayed that she could hear these voices that he knew she loved. Then his own heart jumped as he picked up the high, sweet refrain of one of her favorite songs: *"Do you hear what I hear? . . . Do you hear what I hear?"*

As Danny prayed for God to let Allyson hear, the singers suddenly began the "Hallelujah" chorus. What happened next astounded him. Allyson's eyelids twitched, and he felt a firm squeeze from her hand. Staring into Allyson's face, he thought he saw a tiny half-smile, as thrilling as any smile he had ever seen. Danny Moring wept with relief and knew that he would play the tape over and over. Then someone touched him on the shoulder. It was Allyson's father, pediatrician Dr. Allen Harrell. "Danny," he said gently, "I cannot let you get your hopes up. Allyson can't survive without a miracle." But there was no miracle. Pneumonia set in a few days later, and the illness grew worse.

"The tape made Mrs. Moring smile!" whooped one of the girls when Katherine came into the music room the next day. That spark of hope ignited the students. "There's no way we can *not* have the concert," said one of them. But who would conduct? All eyes were on Katherine Allen. "Never," said Katherine. "I'm not capable of it."

But efforts to find a substitute director failed. One night, Katherine and her mother talked until 1:00 A.M. Over and over, Katherine insisted, "I'm just not a conductor." But she couldn't stop thinking about Mrs. Moring. She remembered the powerful inspiration the teacher brought to their choral group—and the immense satisfaction they felt when she pushed them to their performing limits. The next morning, Katherine announced to her parents, "I've decided to do it."

On December 8, Charleston's magnificent Grace Episcopal Church opened its doors for the Bishop England Christmas concert. Word had spread about the students who were determined to fulfill their teacher's dream. More than five hundred people packed the seats and spilled into the foyer.

In another part of the church, Katherine and the chorus went over the difficult parts one last time. Finally, Katherine called for silence. "We are going to pray together for Mrs. Moring," she said. "And then we're going to go out there and make her proud." As she led the group in the Lord's Prayer, Katherine heard sobs. She struggled for composure herself.

In the darkened sanctuary of the Gothic church, the chorus, holding candles and singing "0 Holy Night," made its way down the aisles. When the singers reached the front, the lights came up. Katherine could see Mrs. Moring's family in the front rows, their faces shining with the same hope the singers felt.

Steadying herself, she looked out over the crowd and informed them that their director was deathly ill. "We dedicate this concert to Mrs. Moring in the hope that she will get well," she said. Then Katherine turned and, with great flair, began the performance. As the voices intoned the familiar Christmas hymns, her confidence rose. But one thought continued to nag her: Could she keep them together for the finale? When the powerful opening to the "Hallelujah" chorus burst from the organ, Katherine took a deep breath and raised her arms. There was an excruciating pause. Then she flung her arms wide—and heard the voices explode, every note in place, warm and confident. Mrs. Moring's students were summoning sounds so pure that Handel's long crescendo of "hallelujahs" seemed to soar to the rafters, touching ears and hearts with the sound of heaven itself.

When silence finally fell, the listeners rose and broke into applause, some weeping and others crowding forward to embrace the singers. Exhausted, Katherine felt a hug at her waist. It was the Morings' little daughter, Elizabeth, embracing her as tightly as she could. Looking into the child's slate-blue eyes, Katherine was overcome with joy.

That same night, less than a mile from the church, Danny Moring sat holding his wife's hand, the tape made by her students still playing. Allyson's condition remained hopeless. Danny didn't even know whether the news of the successful Christmas concert had penetrated her unconsciousness. But slowly, remarkably, over the next few days, her systems began to stabilize. Lungs and kidneys started functioning. Allyson began to recover.

On Christmas morning, just seventeen days after the concert, Allyson sat quietly in her own living room. Baby Robert squirmed in her lap as Danny and Elizabeth fetched presents from beneath the tree. Allyson was bone thin and exhausted, but her face wore a radiant smile. Why she got well, or even when the precise turning point came, is not important to Allyson Moring. The key fact is that her long, tortured slumber was filled with music. "What I remember is music, music, music—the beautiful music and voices that I loved."

Soon after Mrs. Moring got home, Katherine Allen and several others from the choral group tapped gingerly on her door, bearing gifts and flowers. There was an explosion of emotion as the girls and Mrs. Moring hugged one another. She told the girls what she had told so many—that the entire experience has certified her faith in God's power through music and prayer and the wonderful capacity of young people.

Today Allyson Moring, completely recovered, is busy putting final touches on this year's Bishop England Christmas concert. If the most precious of God's gifts is life, the Morings have realized a blessing every bit as special to them as Allyson's recovery—a baby boy born to them in October. Merry Christmas, Mrs. Moring.

—ALLYSON MORING
Charleston, South Carolina
As told to Henry Hurt

Icy Water Rescue

T WAS SATURDAY, DECEMBER 28, 1996. My best friend, Candi
Peterson, and I were on Christmas vacation from the fifth grade,
and had been having a wonderful time. The winter weather had
been unusually harsh, and the night before it had snowed about two
feet in our little town of La Conner, Washington, on the Puget Sound. Snow is
rare where we live: It only comes once every few years. I'd spent the night at
Candi's, and we viewed the situation with delight. The snow seemed like a last-
minute Christmas present from God!

As soon as we were up that morning, we climbed into our heavy snowsuits
and headed outside with a sled. First we went sledding down the hill by Candi's
house. Then we headed over to sled on the small hills of the golf course, next to
the marina. The water at the marina was covered in a thin layer of ice and
looked really cool—we just had to get a closer look. The docks were off limits
to us—we knew we should have an adult and life jackets to go down to the
docks and be around the boats, but all we planned to do was look at the icy
water. It seemed safe enough.

As we started down the ramp, I got a little scared because the docks were
covered with snow. It was hard to see where the sides of the ramp ended, but I
kept on going. We sat down on the narrow, snow-covered dock and put the sled
out on the ice to see if it would break—it didn't. We moved to another part of
the dock to test it again—we wanted to see the ice break! The ice wouldn't

break there either, so we ended our science experiment and decided to go back and sled at the golf course as we'd originally planned. I got up and turned around to leave. But as Candi got up to leave, her feet slipped off the dock, pitching her into the icy water.

I heard the splash, turned around, and screamed, "Candi!" She was in the cold, slushy water a few feet off the dock, trying hard to keep her head above water. I ran back to her, not thinking about anything except that she would die if I couldn't get her out. I lay down on my stomach and managed to grab her hands but I didn't have the strength to pull her out. She was so heavy, weighed down by a snowsuit and heavy boots. We both screamed for help, but no one was around to hear us. I tried again to pull her out but just couldn't get her out of the water. I asked her if she could hold on while I ran for help. "No," she said. "Please don't leave me, Holly."

Her boots had come off under the water by now, and her teeth were chattering. She was very cold.

I stood up and looked around the docks behind me one more time, hoping to see an adult with the strength to pull her out. There was no one. Realizing that I was Candi's only hope, I lay down on the dock to try again to pull her out.

My two earlier attempts to pull Candi out had left me exhausted and my arms aching. I knew that I had only one more try before she drowned. So I closed my eyes for a fraction of a second and prayed. I prayed that I would have the strength to pull my best friend out of the water. And suddenly, I could feel the presence of someone else there with me, someone who would give me the strength and courage to save my friend's life.

In an effort to keep from falling in myself, I hooked my foot under a rope cleat on the dock to give myself a solid anchor. Candi was farther away from the dock now. I could no longer reach her hands, but by stretching out as far as I could, I managed to grab the end of her wool scarf floating on the surface. I said another prayer and I pulled, and despite the fact that the first two tries had left me feeling weak, this time I seemed to get stronger and stronger as I worked. Slowly I pulled her out of the water and onto the dock. I unzipped her snowsuit and pulled her wet clothes off. Growing up around the water, I knew all about hypothermia and how quickly it could happen. Candi and I were both sobbing with relief now, but she was still freezing cold and frightened. I put her on the sled and pulled her up the ramp as quickly as I could to find a public phone. We found one; I called the operator and, still crying, told her our troubles. She put me through to Candi's mother Cheri. Due to the snow and ice, Cheri couldn't bring her car down the hill and had to run down the hill in order to find us. As we waited for her help, I tried to keep Candi as warm as I could by wrapping her in my coat and hugging her. When Candi's mom arrived, we both pulled Candi up the hill on her sled to her house. Cheri immediately put Candi into a hot bath to warm her up.

Candi did not suffer any ill effects from her ordeal. Later, when she and I talked about what had happened, she said that she had felt sure that she was going to die there in the icy water. I told her about my prayers, and that I knew that there was someone watching over us out there that day. Instead of getting weaker from pulling, I had gotten stronger. A big topic at United Methodist, the church my family attends in La Conner, is guardian angels. I just know that there was a guardian angel our there on the dock that day, helping me save Candi.

—HOLLY DeGROOT
La Conner, Washington

Note: Holly, age twelve, was later given a certificate for bravery by the Swinomish Police Department for her icy water rescue.

The Gold and Ivory Tablecloth

AT CHRISTMASTIME MEN AND WOMEN everywhere gather in their churches to wonder anew at the greatest miracle the world has ever known. But the story I like to recall was not a miracle—not exactly.

It happened to a pastor who was very young. His church was very old. Once, long ago, it had flourished. Famous men had preached from its pulpit, prayed before its altar. Rich and poor alike had worshiped there and built it hopefully. Now the good days had passed from the section of town where it stood. But the young pastor and his wife believed in their run-down church. They felt that with paint, hammer, and faith they could get it into shape. Together they went to work.

But late in December a severe storm whipped through the area and the worst blow fell on the little church. A huge chunk of rain-soaked plaster fell out of the inside wall just behind the altar. Sorrowfully the pastor and his wife swept away the mess, but they couldn't hide the ragged hole.

The pastor looked at it and had to remind himself quickly, "Thy will be done!" But his wife wept, "Christmas is only two days away!"

That afternoon the dispirited couple attended an auction held for the benefit of a youth group. The auctioneer opened a box and shook out of its folds a handsome gold and ivory lace tablecloth. It was a magnificent item, nearly fifteen feet long. But it, too, dated from a long-vanished era. Who, today, had any use for such a thing? There were a few halfhearted bids. Then the pastor was seized with what he thought was a great idea. He bought it for $6.50.

He carried the cloth back to the church and tacked it up on the wall behind the altar. It completely hid the hole! And the extraordinary beauty of its shimmering handwork cast a fine holiday glow over the chancel. It was a great triumph. Happily he went back to preparing his Christmas sermon.

Just before noon on Christmas Eve, as the pastor was opening the church, he noticed a woman standing in the cold at the bus stop.

"The bus won't be here for forty minutes," he called, and he invited her into the church to get warm.

She told him that she had come from the city that morning to be interviewed for a job as governess to the children of one of the wealthy families in town but she had been turned down. A war refugee, her English was imperfect.

The woman sat down in the pew and chafed her hands and rested. After a while she dropped her head and prayed. She looked up as the pastor began to adjust the great gold and ivory lace cloth across the hole. She rose suddenly and walked up the steps of the chancel. She looked at the tablecloth. The pastor smiled and started to tell her about the storm damage, but she didn't seem to listen. She took up a fold of the cloth and rubbed it between her fingers.

"It is mine!" she said. "It is my banquet cloth!" She lifted up a corner and showed the surprised pastor that there were initials monogrammed on it. "My husband had the cloth made especially for me in Brussels! There could not be another like it!"

For the next few minutes the woman and the pastor talked excitedly together.

She explained that she was Viennese; that she and her husband had opposed the Nazis and decided to leave the country. They were advised to go separately. Her husband put her on a train for Switzerland. They planned that he would join her as soon as he could arrange to ship their household goods across the border.

She never saw him again. Later she heard that he had died in a concentration camp.

"I have always felt that it was my fault—to leave without him," she said. "Perhaps these years of wandering have been my punishment."

The pastor tried to comfort her, urged her to take the cloth. She refused. Then she went away.

As the church began to fill on Christmas Eve, it was clear that the cloth was going to be a great success. It had been skillfully designed to look its best by candlelight.

After the service, the pastor stood in the doorway; many people told him that the church looked beautiful. One gentle-faced, middle-aged man—he was the local watch and clock repairman—looked rather puzzled.

"It is strange," he said in his soft accent. "Many years ago my wife—God rest her—and I owned such a cloth. In our home in Vienna, my wife put it on the table"—and here he smiled—"only when the bishop came to dinner."

The pastor became very excited. He told the jeweler about the woman who had been in the church earlier in the day.

The startled jeweler clutched the pastor's arm. "Can it be? Does she live?"

Together the two got in touch with the family who had interviewed her. Then, in the pastor's car, they started for the city. And as Christmas Day was born, this man and his wife—who had been separated through the many saddened Yuletides—were reunited.

To all who heard this story, the joyful purpose of the storm that had knocked a hole in the wall of the church was now quite clear. Of course, people said it was a miracle, but I think you will agree it was the season for it!

—REV. HOWARD C. SCHADE
Nyack, New York

Second Chance

HRISTMAS HAS ALWAYS BEEN a very special time of year for the McKinnon household. We didn't always have a lot of gifts, but the holiday had deeper meaning for us than just opening presents. Christmas was about family get-togethers with music, laughter, and feasting on our mother's wonderful cooking after our father's prayer of thanksgiving.

December 1977 looked to be no different. Preparations were well under way for another great family get-together, and everyone wondered excitedly who would draw whose name in our gift selection game. On December 15, my sixty-five-year-old mother Lula told me her doctor wanted her to check into the hospital to investigate her irregular heartbeat. Nothing serious, she assured me. It was just routine.

As I drove her to the hospital, my mother remembered something about the previous August when my wife, Patrice, and I came to my mother and father to tell them the news that we were expecting our first child. I'm not sure why, but as Mother spoke, a dark thought occurred to me: My own grandmother Ellen had died shortly before *my* birth. Would the same fate await our unborn child's grandmother?

The day after Mother checked in, I was shocked to get a call that I should go to the hospital as soon as possible. The young woman from patient services was compassionate as she led me to Mother's physician. I had faced many crisis situations during my military and law enforcement careers. But there is little one can do to prepare for the moment a doctor tells you that your mother has suffered two heart atracks and a stroke.

I thought it might be a bad dream. She'd only been at the hospital overnight for some tests. How could this happen in the hospital? My sister Gloria arrived and I listened again as the doctor explained that our mother wasn't responding. He suggested that we speak to her; perhaps the sound of her children's voices could bring her out of it.

Entering the critical care unit we saw tubes protruding from Mother's nose and mouth, and machines bleeping away, monitoring her feeble life signs. Gloria turned away. "I can't see her this way," she said. I approached the bed, grabbed my mother's hand, and called her name repeatedly. I got no response. I tried again and again. My frustration showed, and the doctor pulled us away to deliver more grim news.

"In her condition and at her age, there is a strong possibility that she may not recover," he said as kindly as he could. His calm professionalism put me at ease and helped me steel myself for telling the rest of the family. I asked the doctor if there was anything I could do to help. "Pray for a Christmas miracle," he said.

I drifted down the corridor, trying to gather my thoughts. I stumbled into the hospital chapel, slid into a short pew, and began to pray. For the next several days, I would arrive at my mother's bedside, grasp her hand, and talk to her. I told her how Patrice's pregnancy was going and what I thought about my job with the police department. After an hour or more, I'd retreat to the chapel where the family gathered: my sisters Gloria, Ada, Helen, Bernice, and, of course, our father, Cota McKinnon.

My father's prayers were always out loud. Father, the head deacon at Weeping Willow Baptist Church, would ask for his wife's recovery and always end by saying, "I pray for Jesus' sake."

Two days before Christmas, I got a call from Gloria. She was exuberant. "Guess what? Ma is up and talking," she said, almost hyperventilating. I dropped the phone and hurried over. Ma was propped up in the hospital bed and seemed to be having a wonderful time talking to everyone.

She spoke of losing weight. She couldn't wait to get home and fix her own meals because she didn't like hospital food. She knew she wouldn't be home in time for our Christmas Day celebration, but she gave explicit instructions to my sisters about how to fix Father's favorite Christmas meal. When I saw my mother's doctor, he said, "Maybe this is your miracle."

It was an incredible day. All of us had given up hope that we'd ever speak with our mother again, yet there she was, being her usual animated self. We all went home feeling blessed. Early the next morning, Christmas Eve, yet another phone call came from the hospital. "Get back here immediately," they said.

When I got there, the doctor's head was low. "You've got bad news," I said.

"Yes," the doctor said. "Your mother just passed." As the rest of the family began arriving and tears began to flow, I thought about how I'd hoped for a Christmas miracle that would save Mother. And in the sadness that engulfed our family that day, it slowly occurred to me that indeed we had had our miracle. Our mother had been gone, but she had come back to us for one full joyous day. Our entire family had had a second chance to share our love with our mother. That was our miracle.

—ISAIAH MCKINNON
Chief, Detroit Police Department

The Kiss

N MY FAIR LADY, the arrogant but charming Henry Higgins attempts to teach Eliza an important lesson when he says, "The greatest secret, Eliza...is in having the same manners for all human souls; in short, behaving as though you were in heaven, where there are no third-class carriages, and one soul is as good as another." For most of us, it is easy to love those we admire and those who return our affection, but the big test in life comes in caring for those who are somewhat difficult to love and who give nothing in return—the stranger, the less powerful, the poor, the unimportant. I learned that lesson one Christmas many years ago when we lived in California.

I was in charge of a woman's organization in my church for several years. Part of my responsibility was to look after the sick and elderly, giving compassionate service to those in need.

I was told there was a woman in our area who was unable to attend church because of health problems and who needed some assistance. Two other women from the church joined me to visit her to see how we could help her. Margaret was a small Danish woman with a slight accent, almost blind from diabetes and very arthritic. She lived alone and had two grown children who hardly ever came to see her. From the minute we met her, we could sense that she was a very proud and independent woman, and that she was uncomfortable and embarrassed to ask for our help. She had owned her own business for many years—a very fine dress shop—and a few of the beautiful wedding gowns she sold still hung in plastic bags in her closets. Despite her rather cold and formal demeanor, we could see that she badly needed our assistance.

We spent many days there over the next year. We would come in the morning and straighten her apartment; then we would fix lunch and try to leave something for her dinner. She would thank us very properly, never showing any real emotion; we sensed she had grown lonely and bitter over the years and had learned to keep herself at a distance from the rest of the world. We tried very hard to be caring and loving, but we always left wondering if she even appreciated anything we had done. All in all, it was not a very gratifying experience; Margaret simply would not let us love her.

Time went on, Margaret's health deteriorated, and finally she was put into a nursing home. I hadn't seen her for some months and was feeling a little guilty about it. It was December and I was caught up in the mad dash of the holiday season: parties, shopping, Christmas cards, decorating, and many other activities to squeeze in before the big day. My sisters and I had been invited to a Christmas luncheon, an annual event I looked forward to each year. It was a very elegant affair in Beverly Hills and it was fun to get dressed up and mingle with some of the well-known people who attended. On this particular December day, however, I had a nagging feeling that I needed to cancel my luncheon plans and instead pay a visit to Margaret. As I dutifully walked from my parked car to her drab-looking nursing home, I kept wondering what had compelled me to give up my favorite party to visit a woman I didn't really know or even particularly like. I was full of resentment and was feeling a bit like a martyr. I certainly wasn't doing this act of kindness for the right reasons.

My own mother had lived the last five years of her life in a nursing home, stricken with such severe arthritis that she remained in a fetal position most of the time. I had spent many hours there visiting her; now the all-too-familiar smells and sounds of another nursing home brought back bittersweet memories. As I stood by Margaret's bedside and looked down at her face, she reminded me very much of my own mother, who was half Danish—the same fair complexion and very blue eyes. As I reflected on my mother for a moment, I remembered what I used to do When I visited her. I asked Margaret if I could put lotion on her hands.

"Oh, please do," she quietly answered. I began to massage her thin, gnarled hands that looked so much like my mother's. Then I put a little lotion on her face and neck and rubbed some on her back. I picked up a brush and brushed her white hair and tried to make it look pretty. She began to relax and seemed to enjoy the attention and intimacy, something I thought this proud and unfriendly woman could never do.

Suddenly as I was rubbing more lotion on her arms, she grabbed my hand and looked up at me with her weary old eyes. "Kiss me," she whispered. "Kiss me." A little surprised, I smiled, leaned down, and kissed her softly. Then she said, "Oh, again, please." I kissed her on the other cheek and I noticed tears in her eyes. It was as if my simple kisses were melting away the layers of cold, hard exterior that had built up over all her years of loneliness. I suddenly found myself kissing her again and again all over her face as we cried together. I gave her a warm embrace that she desperately clung to and I assured her I'd come back again soon. As I turned to go, the realization dawned on me: Here was an old woman whose children had all but abandoned her, but whose hunger for the human touch was so intense that she would reach out to a mere acquaintance for any loving gesture that could feed her starving soul. At that moment, I felt honored to be the one to meet that need.

I walked out of the hospital on cloud nine, feeling like I had been transformed. The pure joy of the true Christmas spirit filled my heart and soul as it never had before. I now realized why I had decided to forgo my luncheon that day: There were more important people to be with and lives to touch than would ever be possible in an elegant restaurant filled with celebrities. I wasn't sure why I had felt such an urgency about the matter—perhaps the urgency was for me.

I remember a story I once heard, in which one of the innkeepers who couldn't find room for Joseph and Mary on that first Christmas night, later said in his own defense, "What could be done? The inn was full of folk—and there were just two of them—no servants, just a workman sort of man leading a donkey and his wife thereon, drooping and pale. I saw them not myself, my servants having driven them away; but if I had seen them, how was I to know? Should innkeepers welcome stragglers in all our towns from Beersheba to Dan, in case He should come? There was a sign, they say, a heavenly light resplendent, but I had no time for stars; and there were songs of angels in the air out on the hills. But how was I to hear amid the thousand clamors of an inn?"

Fortunately for me that day, I had put the clamors of the world aside, and for a few brief moments had witnessed the star's heavenly light and felt the angels' song. The memory of that kiss planted on a weary old woman's sweet face, cultivated by human tears, has grown and enlarged each new Christmas with a love for all mankind that I never knew possible. I had learned for myself that the gift of a loving heart at Christmas is truly the greatest gift of all.

—OLIVIA PRATT
Bronxville, New York

The Gift

HIS PAST CHRISTMAS I received an extraordinary gift, a miraculous and selfless gift from someone I barely knew. For many years I have had lupus, and last year my doctors told me that as a result of the lupus my kidneys were failing. I was facing a future in which thrice-weekly dialysis would become a fact of life, unless I underwent a kidney transplant. My family and friends rallied around me and took medical tests in order to determine whether any of them could donate a healthy kidney. After many weeks of forms and tests, we received the crushing news that, because of my O-positive blood type, no one I knew was a potential kidney donor for me. "We will add you right away to the list of kidney patients in the country awaiting transplants," my medical team told me. "But the wait could be as long as three years. Your kidneys will fail long before that." I was devastated by that news, and even more disheartened to hear on the car radio that same day of the sudden death of humorist Erma Bombeck during a kidney transplant operation.

Despite this grim news I still needed to take care of the small chores that are a part of everyday living, and so it was that I went into the bank to make a deposit, still reeling from the information I'd received. "Miki, are you all right?" my favorite bank teller asked me. My sad tale rushed out of me there in the bank lobby. I unloaded detail after detail to a woman I barely knew. We'd chatted casually over the three years I'd banked at that branch, mainly about art.

I am a painter and the bank teller is a dancer, so we'd connected as artists in some small way, but she knew nothing of my medical struggles.

"And no one in my family is a match! I could wait three years before a kidney is found for me!" She sympathized over my plight and asked a few polite questions about the transplant process before I finished up my banking business and a went on to the next errand.

Several weeks later I met again with my doctors to discuss the situation. "So," they said, smiling broadly, "tell us about your donor!"

"Donor? I don't have a donor, you know that. No one was a match for me."

The head doctor looked confused, and looked down at some papers he held. "Yes, we have it right here. Mary Groves is her name."

"I don't know anyone named Mary Groves," I protested.

"Yes," the doctors insisted, "Mary Groves. It says here that she is your bank teller and a dancer."

And then it hit me. "Oh my God!" I burst out crying, suddenly remembering that day in the bank when I'd told her about my situation. What on earth had inspired her to decide that she, a woman who barely knew me, would willingly undergo major surgery and donate one of her healthy kidneys to me?

Mary told me that she felt she'd been chosen to help me. "God is providing for you through me," she said. "I'm receiving this as a gift, too—I'm getting to do this for you. This is a God-given thing, when He asks you to do something He gives you the tools to do it—the people and the peace of mind."

After many more months of testing (it was a match!) and soul-searching, the transplant took place in San Francisco on December 10, 1996. We both sailed through, even though as the donor the surgery was more invasive for Mary than it was for me. We met incredible people there in the transplant unit of the hospital. The walls were hung with photographs of folks smiling and hugging each other—loving pairs of people just like us who had gone through this procedure together.

Mary and I have a special bond, after all we've been through together. My dream is that we will someday be able to mount an exhibition together; I will do the abstract paintings and Mary will dance. I want to get her name out into the world—Mary Groves—to let everyone know how special she is and what she has done. Her generosity and my life-and-death experience have changed my whole outlook on life. No matter how horrible the news is on television, I know that there are special people in the world like Mary Groves, people who are guardian angels for the rest of us.

—Miki Hsu Leavey
Napa, California

Ten-Candy-Bar Christmas

T WAS 1987, and my girls and I were going to have our first Christmas together since we'd become a single-parent family. And we were broke.

The fact that we could pay our monthly bills was cause a for celebration—but there would be no extras that year. I explained to my daughters that we could afford a bare Christmas tree, but that, for the first time in their young lives, there would be no gifts underneath it. "This is going to be a Top Ramen and Kool-Aid Christmas, girls," I explained. We were poor but we were happy, and the three of us set about making ornaments out of paper scraps and aluminum foil to brighten up the way our bare apartment looked.

I'd been taking the bus to work (the old family car could go only so far), and a few days before Christmas my girls came down to the bus stop to meet me, faces shining with excitement. "There's a turkey raffle, Mom! We heard about it on the radio and we called up and entered! I bet we win the turkey—you just wait and see!" Such sweet little optimists they were, not yet worn out by life's bad luck as I was. I smiled and patted them on their shoulders and agreed that, yes, it would be wonderful if we won the turkey mentioned on the radio.

I went to work as usual on Christmas Eve. Mine was not what you would call a challenging job, but it kept a roof over our heads during those tough times. Not much happened at work on the day before Christmas. Most of the other employees had taken the day off to do a little last-minute shopping and the office was very quiet. Midway through the day the phone rang. "Cathe, it's for you," the receptionist said. "Somebody from a radio station." We'd won the turkey after all! The girls and I hauled that big, cold bird home on the bus, singing Christmas carols and giggling the whole way back to the apartment.

The apartment complex that we lived in that year was filled with other mothers in the same financial situation as I, with not much other than the love we had for our kids to keep us warm at night. So we decided to invite some of the other single moms and their kids to join us for our feast of—you guessed it—roast turkey, Top Ramen, and KoolAid. It was a wonderful meal we all shared together.

After the dishes had been cleared and the girls had gone off to visit friends in another apartment, I heard a light tap on our door. I opened it. No one was there. An envelope fell to the ground; it had been stuck in the door frame. No note, no greeting, but inside the envelope were two worn dollar bills. I suspected that this was the only way one of the other moms knew to thank us for sharing the Christmas turkey. I looked up and down the hallway for a hint of our benefactor, but all of the doors were closed tight. Suddenly, I had a wild idea.

With the girls occupied for the next hour or two, I slipped on my coat and headed out to the local discount store—the "ninety-eight-cent store." I raced down in the hope that it was still open this late at night—and yes! It was! I could hardly contain my zeal as I cruised the aisles, trying to decide how to stretch my two dollars into the best Christmas gifts I could. And then I saw the candy aisle. I never let the girls have candy, so this would be a crazy surprise. With my two dollars I was able to buy twenty candy bars—ten for each of my daughters.

I ran home, hoping they were still out. Searching the apartment for gift wrap I came up empty-handed, but I did find plenty of typing paper. I pulled out the kids' crayons and decorated the paper to my heart's content, carefully drawing gold and silver stars and Christmas trees to make it look as festive as possible. And then I wrapped each one of those twenty candy bars into a miniature Christmas gift and spread them all out underneath the homely little tree. It looked like Santa had come after all.

When the girls came home, they shouted with delight to see gifts under the tree. "Don't get too excited now, it's all I could afford...." But the girls carried on with such joy at every candy bar they unwrapped that you would have thought they were opening the best toys F.A.O. Schwarz had to offer. We hugged and laughed and sat down at the table together to share the candy bars and continue our holiday feast.

We awakened Christmas morning with loving hearts and the miracle of each other, together and happy despite all we'd been through with the divorce that year. My girls and I have never forgotten our "ten-candy-bar Christmas" and the magical appearance of, first, a turkey, and then, two dollars, which made it such a special time.

—CATHE ODOM
Sacramento, California

Homeless Santa

CRUMMY 1988 WAS WINDING DOWN as my roommate Margaret Cable and I set out for an afternoon snack on Christmas Eve. I'd just returned to California after a dark three months of hiding in the Swedish woods in my own private Ingmar Bergman film after the breakup of a long-term romance. My arrival home had been as dramatic as my sudden departure some months before. I was booked on a Pan Am flight from London to San Francisco. Having been away from home for three months, I was so anxious to get home for Christmas that I told myself if I missed the flight I would take the next available flight, Pan Am 103. I made my flight with just minutes to spare. Passengers for the San Francisco flight were checking in at a counter directly across from the New York flight, but I absentmindedly got into the wrong line with the New York—bound folks. When I noticed my mistake, I joked about it to the people in line and made my way across the room.

As my parents drove home from the airport over slow-moving California freeways, they told me about the midair explosion of Flight 103 over Lockerbee, Scotland. "But I saw those people," I said. "How can they all be dead?" My dreams that night were haunted by the image of the Scottish countryside strewn with carefully packed Christmas gifts, steamed puddings from Harrod's, and little piles of Christmas candy that an airport Santa had handed to everyone waiting in line to go through the security X ray.

After such a close brush with death I was feeling a little peculiar on that bright California afternoon, a little tentative and oddly disconnected to what was going on around me. I'd come home after an absence of three months, but I didn't feel like I'd come back in one piece.

Craving the taste of authentic Mexican food, Margaret and I chose to head for a ramshackle burrito house in a dicey part of town. Near the train tracks and several homeless shelters, it was not a part of town you'd expect to find two middle-class girls visiting on Christmas Eve. We ordered our burritos and sat outside in the sun. The streets around us were deserted; office workers and commuters had gone home to get an early start on the holiday.

Margaret nudged my arm. "Oh great," she said. "Looks like we're about to get hit up for money." A disheveled man was making his way toward us through the parking lot of the burrito house, his progress slowed both by his age and by the oversized green sack he carried on his back. His hair was long and snowy white, his thick beard spread over the top of his tattered jacket. Margaret and I clucked our tongues and shook our heads and began to search our pockets for loose change in order to dispense with him quickly and get on with our meal.

Slowly and quietly he made his way across the blacktop until he was standing in front of us. He stopped, and without saying a word he rolled his heavy bag off his shoulder and set it on the ground before us. Untying the top, he reached in and began to rummage through the contents of his bag. Margaret and I watched as he found what he was seeking and removed his hand. He held a shiny red apple. In total silence and with great dignity he held the apple out to Margaret. She reached out and accepted his gift. He reached into his green duffel bag again and this time pulled out a Snickers bar and offered it to me. "No," I said. "We can't take your food; you need it." Margaret and I both held our new gifts back out to him. "We can't take your food." The man smiled shyly and shook his head. "I can't eat it. My teeth are no good. Merry Christmas."

He would not accept the money we tried to give him that afternoon; he just kept quietly shaking his head and smiling as we tried to press dollar bills into his hand. Finally, he agreed to the purchase of a cup of coffee for him. He took the steaming Styrofoam container and, shouldering his bag once again, continued on his way.

I think about that homeless man whenever I pass down that street. I think about the quiet man with the big white beard and the bag of presents who gave two privileged girls part of the only food he had. The spirit of giving is all around us and can come upon us so unexpectedly. We need to be able to give back what we can to those who need it most.

—JENNIFER BASYE SANDER
Granite Bay, California

The Secret Dolls

HAD BEEN A SINGLE MOTHER for years, raising five sons. Now I was remarried to David, a widower, and I was feeling a little awkward in David's family home. Making the adjustment was a challenge for both me and my new family, which included David's three grown-up daughters.

As December approached, I felt apprehensive when I thought of the holidays. None of my own children would make it home for Christmas, and I wanted David's children to know that I loved them and was happy to be a part of their family. What could I give them?

When we had first gotten married in September, I had begun investigating and reorganizing the house so I would know where things were and so I would feel more at home. One day, I found an old shoebox covered with dust. Inside, packed in shredded newspapers, were parts for three porcelain dolls. I was startled and pleased. I knew that David's first wife, Lois, had loved working with ceramics. Her daughter-in-law once mentioned that Lois had even begun some ceramic dolls for her three daughters, but the figures had never been finished. Were these the dolls Lois had begun?

I thought of David's daughters and my longing to be their friend. Could I somehow finish the dolls and present them as a Christmas gift, not only from me but from their own loving mother? Ecstatic, I told David of my discovery, and he shared my excitement. First, I took the dolls to Linda, a doll expert whom a friend had recommended. She was astonished at the delicate pieces and agreed to finish them by painting and firing the ceramic parts, assembling the dolls, and making dresses. I chose dress colors that I thought matched each daughter's personality. Each doll would have a slightly different shade of auburn hair.

Upon my return home, the phone was ringing. It was Linda, her voice filled with emotion. "Do you know these dolls have been dedicated?" she asked me.

"What's a dedicated doll?"

"On each doll's ceramic body appears an inscription: 'To my dear Kathy,' 'To my dear Heidi,' 'To my dear Lorelee.' Each is signed, 'Love, Mom, 1970.'"

Like Lois's hand from the past, I thought. The dedications made the dolls even more precious, and I looked forward to giving them to David's daughters. I now realized that Lois had poured the ceramic parts for those dolls fourteen long years before, when the youngest girl, Lorelee, had been only five years old.

Finally the dolls were ready. I had written a note to each of the girls, telling them about my feelings for them and explaining why the dolls were so important. I emphasized that each doll came from two mothers who loved them a great deal—their own mom and me. I bought gift boxes, nested the dolls in tissue paper, added the notes, and wrapped everything carefully. I was more excited about those dolls than about any other gifts I was giving. So was David.

The next day, we assembled the children, their spouses, the grandchildren, and the cousins for our presentation. Wordlessly, David and I gave each daughter her package. They began unwrapping them. Silence, then gasps, sobs, and floods of tears. Somehow, even Lois seemed to be there.

Lorelee threw her arms around me. Later, Heidi confided that the doll confirmed to her that I was supposed to be part of their family circle. Kathy wrote a note expressing how touched she was and how meaningful the doll would always be to her. And through this gift of love from Lois and myself, I finally felt the acceptance and the comfort of being a real part of David's family.

—MARGENE B. LYON
Salt Lake City, Utah

My Shiny Fire Truck

IKE MOST CHILDREN, I asked for toys every Christmas. But the most memorable present for me was the bright red fire engine that came Christmas Eve 1970. Now this big, red hook and ladder was not in a box or decorated with a bow. It was, however, waiting for me when I got home.

Every Christmas Eve my whole family bundled up and went to midnight Mass. This particular year, my little sister was home with the chicken pox. She had such a high fever and outbreak of sores that my father decided to stay home with her.

As the rest of us put on our coats, my mother made sure that Dad and Tracy were as comfortable as possible. The lights were turned down or off; goodies on the table were covered; everything was ready for us to go.

I remember that the dining room table looked so beautiful, laden with all the food we were going to eat when we returned. On the mantel was a centerpiece that my mother had received as a gift: four tall red candles surrounded by holly and berries on a plastic base. All the cards and artwork that we children had made circled the candles for a complete holiday theme.

As we drove off, Dad was in his easy chair with a nice fire going, the lights of the Christmas tree filled the room with color, and my sister was asleep on the couch.

Christmas Eve is a wonderful time. Mass, as usual, was overwhelming with the choir, a full congregation, and the priests dressed in magnificent robes. We sang, shared, and prayed. I was hoping that my sister would feel better. I mean, what a time to be sick! Santa was coming; Christ was born; it was a holiday for family, friends, food, and, of course, presents.

My mother, brothers, and I had stopped by our friends' house for some holiday cheer before heading for home. We didn't stay long, knowing that Dad and Tracy were waiting for us. Besides, we always got to open one present before Santa brought us the real loot in the middle of the night. We said our good-byes and sang carols all the way home.

As we were busy singing and trying to remember the words, we braked at the light down the street from our house. In the distance we could see big trucks in the middle of the street. Suddenly, silence descended in our car. Only the pounding of hearts was heard. It was hard to believe what we saw, or what we thought we saw. I think my mother sat through two green lights. We all knew that we should make the sign of the cross if we ever heard or saw a siren because someone might need our prayers—but us? I mean, things like this happen to other people, and how could anything like this possibly happen on Christmas Eve?

As we drew nearer, we realized that those big trucks—those big, bright, red trucks—were in front of our house. The firemen were packing up their gear. On the porch two dark figures stood trembling. Only the whites of their eyes and teeth showed through the soot.

I could feel my knees get weak as I imagined what they were feeling. The tears streaming down their faces began to wash the bits and pieces of soot from their cheeks. Between those tears, my sister tried to tell us what had taken place during the last hour.

The same centerpiece that mother had so carefully placed on the mantel, up and out of reach of young hands, had been left with the candles burning.

Within the time we were gone, the candles had burned down to the holly and berries, melting the plastic base with so much heat that all the cards and artwork had gone up in flames.

My sister awoke to find the room filled with smoke. She tried to call my father's name, but began choking on the fumes. She could hear him coughing nearby, but he was not responding to her cries. She crawled on the floor over to his chair and began shaking him, but he was not coming to. My sister dragged him to the front door and laid him on the cold porch outside. Nine years old and weak from fever, she had had the strength of two men.

One of the neighbors saw the commotion and called for help. Within seconds, the firemen responded to the call. The house was badly damaged by the smoke, but all the walls were still standing and two lives were saved.

The thought of losing another family member was unbearable to us. Several years earlier, we had lost an important member of our close-knit family, and the holidays ever since had always seemed to lack something or someone. As soon as reality hit that, yes, my father and sister were alive and well—dirty but happy to be alive—our natural senses of humor came through. Making jokes at the oddest moments has helped us get through so many rough times. Standing there on the lawn, mother laughed at being blamed for burning the pies again and for not dusting as well as usual. With my family gathered around each other and the firemen looking on, I thanked Santa for giving me the best and biggest fire engine a kid could ever ask for.

—KIT DILLON GIVAS
Carmichael, California

Circle of Love

S WE GROW OLDER, we come to realize that one of the genuine gifts of childhood is the magical way that a small child views even the simplest thing. The memory of opening our first pop-up book, finding the hidden toy in the Cracker Jack box, or riding a bike without training wheels—each of these events seems like magic at the time.

Much of the magic in my early years was provided by the gifts of two glamorous aunts, Aunt Lupe and Aunt Mary. My mother Vivian was one of twelve children of a pear farming family in the Sacramento River Delta. Her sisters lavished toys and attention on my sister and me; we were the sole beneficiaries of their undivided love and devotion.

Aunt Lupe was particularly exotic. She lived in Palm Springs, and to a seven-year-old like me, that seemed the very pinnacle of sophistication and elegance. Her frequent letters and postcards were exciting and colorful and told of fancy parties, perpetually sunny skies and swimsuit weather, and frequent sightings of famous movie stars. Like clockwork, the gifts from Palm Springs would arrive for our birthdays and at Christmas. Her carefully selected gifts brought joy and contentment to our young lives. Someone from far away loved and cherished us, and it made us feel tremendously special.

In the mid-1960s Aunt Lupe truly outdid herself. Showing the sixth sense she seemed to have for our interests, that year she sent us each a beautiful satin-lined ivory jewelry box with hand-painted pink flowers and gold trim. When the box was opened, a delicate plastic ballerina spun around on one foot to the tune of the "Blue Danube Waltz."

But there was an even more wonderful surprise tucked inside the pink satin lining: a piece of costume jewelry, a Christmas pin that was the most perfect thing I had ever seen in my short life—in the shape of an old-fashioned Christmas tree, like a Currier and Ives Christmas card tree, framed by a snow-tinged window on a winter's night. Its enamel branches were laced with "snow," and semiprecious stones were scattered in abundance from top to bottom. The tip of the tree was crowned with a gold star with a crystal in the middle. To this day, I cannot think about that pin without feeling the love and security I felt as a young child, and realizing how fortunate I was to have someone who thought that I was special enough to merit this sparkling treasure. It was pure magic.

Through the years and the Christmas seasons to come, my prized Christmas tree pin was an annual adornment. I pinned it to college blazers, to the red wool cape that I had sewn myself, and to the first grown-up houndstooth suit I purchased to celebrate my appointment to a position by the California governor. I so treasured that pin and the memories it contained of Christmases past that I neither checked my coat nor let it out of my sight during its holiday forays.

In 1988 I attended my boss's Christmas party in the company of the love of my life, Kevin. Naturally I wore my Christmas pin. The combination of pink champagne and my frustration at our unresolved relationship brought the evening to an early and tearful close. I went home that night alone and unhappy.

As I sobbed alone in my house, I decide that if I immediately hung up my party dress and put away my holiday coat and purse, then perhaps I would have no physical memories of this night the following morning. It was as I was hanging up my black velvet duster that I noticed—the Christmas pin that had been with me for almost twenty years, for almost two thirds of my life, was gone.

I searched my car. It was not there. Frantic, I called my boss and asked him to look around his house. No, came the reply ten minutes later; it was not to be found at his house. Despite my broken heart and the 30-degree weather on that foggy night, I pulled a coat on over my flannel nightgown and drove the fifteen miles to my boss's house in my bunny slippers, armed with a flashlight and my prayers that the pin would be lying there on the sidewalk. I searched the surrounding neighborhood for forty-five minutes, but the pin was gone. And gone, too, were my cozy feelings of Christmas love.

The loss of that pin ushered in one of the darkest periods of my life. The breast cancer that had ravaged my beautiful mother for almost ten years was now winning its evil campaign to take her life, and through rivers of tears and counseling I also realized that Kevin and I did not have the kind of future together that I both wanted and deserved. The prospect of those two losses occurring simultaneously in my life was unbearable. I found solace in myriad work projects, but I was scared to death. My father's grief at the approaching loss of his life partner, coupled with Kevin's emotional absence, left me alone to deal with my fears.

The Christmas of 1989 would be the last one we would spend with my mom. Through a miracle of God she was released from the hospital in time to attend Aunt Mary's traditional tamale dinner. I witnessed the joy in her eyes each moment she spent in the company of the family; I am truly grateful for my mom having had the strength to endure what would be her last Christmas season with us. She was storing up her own memories to reflect on during her quiet times in heaven.

My mother left this life just a few short months after that. Despite months of counseling before her death, nothing could have prepared me for the hopelessness I felt following her passing. There were entire days spent in my pajamas. I had lost half of my life base, and I did not know how to continue being the self-assured, ambitious young woman she had raised me to be.

But the darkness of winter passed and spring finally arrived, and with it the annual invitation to visit the beach house of Aunt Mary and Uncle Roger. My childhood was filled with summer memories of white sand, starfish, and walks with my parents on the beaches of Pajaro Dunes. The beach house was the last place I thought I could endure at this moment in my life. But my Aunt Mary began to wear down my objections. She was grieving, too, she pointed out, and returning to the very spot where we had enjoyed so many good times would be therapeutic for us all.

And so I agreed to go. Surprisingly, the drive itself offered peace of mind, and as the odometer registered the passing miles, my sense of tranquillity increased. Maybe Aunt Mary knew something that I didn't, something about facing our fears and healing.

At the beach house that year, Aunt Mary and I found common ground in the love and loss of my mom, her sister. We spent hours sitting on the beach, laughing and crying through our stories and recollections of summers past. On the last day of the trip, I awoke with a sense of rejuvenation. It had been so long since I'd had any energy that I assumed this burst I was feeling was due to the ocean air. I had no idea then that I had passed one of the most important tests of grieving, six months after losing Mom. I had returned to the scene of happy family times and faced painful memories.

The drive back to Sacramento began peacefully. I was in no hurry to get back, as I felt so serene and didn't want to jeopardize this newfound calm. Impulsively I stopped at a little town near Pajaro, a little town where the Main Street consisted of a block of antique shops. It was early morning, and some shops had not yet opened their doors.

The last antique shop on the right side of the street was open for business, though, and as I stepped in, I recognized the musty odor of old furniture and well-used books. Through the maze of Victorian lamps and curio cabinets filled with silver spoons and other standard antique fare, I spotted the jewelry case in the back of the store. Perhaps there was some small trinket there that I could take away to remind me of my newfound strength.

I have always believed that things happen for a reason, and the sight that I then beheld affirmed my beliefs. There, tucked in a corner on an old piece of velvet, was the Christmas tree pin I had lost one year before. I asked the shopkeeper to remove it from the display case and, with trembling hands, turned the little pin over. Yes, this was it; the very same company name was inscribed on the back of the pin! In a miracle of rediscovery, I had found the one tangible thing I valued most, a treasure from my beloved past.

Though there was much work to be done emotionally for me and my family, I was now firmly on the way to healing. The boundlessness of the seashore, with waves breaking one after another for all eternity, and the Christmas pin that held within its branches so many feelings of warmth and love, were again returned to me. In the years to come, I would face other losses and disappointments, but I now knew that I possessed the strength and support from my circle of family and friends that would protect me and sustain my recovery whenever I needed them. And my holiday symbol of love, my Christmas pin, would again accompany me into another year of life.

—VALERIE J. REYNOSO
Sacramento, California

Christmas Doesn't Come
from a Store

IME WAS RUNNING OUT. It was December 24—Christmas Eve—and I still hadn't found that magical feeling, the spirit of Christmas. I had done things I'd thought would bring it on—attended my children's school performance of Christmas carols, decorated our tree, baked, shopped, wrapped. Yet nothing seemed to spark the Christmas spirit within me. I had resigned myself to the fact that this just might not be a very good Christmas.

My husband, Steve, a firefighter, was on his routine twenty-four-hour shift at the firehouse, Which meant he would not be home for either Christmas Eve or Christmas morning. Our four children and I were eager to spend what time we could with him, so we all drove down to the station.

As we arrived, the firefighters had just returned from a first-aid call to a nearby motel, where they had rendered care to a young boy with a fever and other symptoms. My husband expressed to us his feelings of concern and his desire to do something more for the boy and his brother and their mother. They had fled an abusive, alcoholic situation and were now hundreds of miles from home, with one change of clothes each, very little money, and now an ill child on Christmas Eve.

Steve looked at me and at each of our children and asked, "What else can we do to help them? We picked up a small tree on the way back to the station that we want to decorate for them, but what more can we do this late?" It was 9:25 P.M. Our children began a clamor of ideas. My daughter was sure a toy store somewhere was still open. I didn't share her hope, largely because even if we did find a store open, I didn't know how we would pay for anything we found.

I wanted to share as much as my children did, but this Christmas was already our leanest ever. Our own children were receiving only two gifts each. Still, we drove around eagerly looking for anything that might be open, planning to meet Steve and the other firefighters back at the motel room before the little family returned from the hospital, where they'd gone for medical care. Every store we saw was closed. Then one of my sons said, "Hey, I know somewhere that's open."

"Yeah, and they've got presents already wrapped!" declared the other one. Wondering what they were talking about, I pulled the car to the side of the street, and in frustration I turned to the kids and asked, "Oh yeah. Just where is this great place?" Their answer was so enthusiastic and genuine that it instantly ignited within me the flame of the Christmas spirit. "We can go to our house," they chimed together. "The presents are already wrapped and under the tree."

I asked them if they really wanted to do this, and their eager response was, "Yes. Yes! Now hurry!" Once we were home, I watched with wonder as they pulled name tags off of their presents and picked certain ornaments from our tree. At first, I was surprised to see that the ornaments they picked were the ones they themselves had made over the years. Then I realized that they were giving of themselves, and that these ornaments had special value.

Two of my boys came out of their bedroom with their baseball gloves, their "pride and joy" mitts. We loaded up the presents, some tree lights, and the candy and other goodies that served as our family's stocking stuffers, and then headed back to the motel. The manager let us into the austere little room, and we set right to work with the firefighters, who had also brought gifts.

We set the tree on the tablerop and adorned it with lights and the ornaments. Some of the firefighters hung candy bars and twenty-dollar bills on it with paper clips. Presents were placed under the tree, canned goods were stacked in the corner, and clothes for the mother and children were folded neatly on the nightstand. The room was transformed.

On each of the bed pillows lay a somewhat used baseball glove from our boys, and I saw my fifteen-year-old place between the mitts one of his most prized possessions. It was his home run baseball, which had been awarded to him after he had hit it in a home run. I doubted that the little boys receiving this prize could possibly know what a sacrifice this was or what a revered spot that ball had held in my son's room for the past six months. But that moment I knew that in my son's heart, the spirit of Christmas flamed brightly, lighting that little room even after we turned off all the lights except the diamondlike ones on the tree.

I had almost given up on finding that precious spirit of Christmas. But it was given to me by my dear husband, who recognized a need when he saw it, and by my children, who so eagerly responded. I realized as never before that the Christmas spirit comes to us most abundantly as we give ourselves to others.

—SANDI SCHUREMAN
Mesa, Arizona

An All-American Christmas

T IS NOT OFTEN that we are given the chance in life to help another who really needs it. Because I lived in a comfortable suburban neighborhood surrounded for blocks in all directions by families that looked just like mine, the chances seemed remote that I would ever do anything that would have an impact on the future of a needy family. But I did, and it was truly a Christmas miracle.

I met Lupe through our parish priest at church. A single mother with six children ranging in age from six to seventeen, she had gone to the church to ask for suggestions on finding a job. Our priest knew that I ran a day care center at my home and was on the lookout for a full-time helper. He arranged a Saturday interview for her, and, recognizing a loving and kind woman who would work well with the children, I hired her.

We soon established a daily routine: She would find a ride to work, and at the end of the day I would drive her the short mile home. The contrast between the coziness of my house and the simplicity of hers was heartbreaking. Lupe lived with her children in a small house only minutes from my neighborhood, but her house contained only one mattress and a few chairs, since the winter before had been a rainy one and roof leaks had ruined most of the furniture and all of the other mattresses. Lupe and her children were sleeping on a concrete floor when I first met her. Through word of mouth and the help of some of my friends, we were able to find enough bedding for her children and a brand-new bed for her.

Over the months, I got to know Lupe very well. Although we did not speak the same language, I knew that she was a woman of pride, a very good mother who was willing to work hard to provide for her family. Her situation was not the stereotype of the lazy welfare family, so frequently portrayed in the press. Lupe was the sole supporter of the family that her husband had deserted. She had emigrated from Mexico with her husband more than a decade before and had obtained her citizenship in 1995, a fact of which she was very proud. Her children, however, were all considered illegal immigrants.

One winter day Lupe came to work very upset. When I learned the extent of her problems, I understood her emotional state. She had begun the complicated process of obtaining citizenship for her children, but after filling out the paperwork and paying application fees she had hit an enormous snag—since the children were considered illegal immigrants, she would have to pay a fine on each child before the citizenship process could be completed. The fine for each one of her six children was $650, a total of $3,900. And now that the process had begun and deadlines had been set, she could very well see her children deported to Mexico if she didn't pay the money.

I calmed Lupe down as best I could and called the immigration office to sort out what she was telling me. The situation was just as she'd described it—if she paid the fines, the children's applications for citizenship would go forward; if she didn't pay the fines, the children could be deported.

In addition to working during the week for me, Lupe and her children were already working weekends at the local farmer's market. There was literally no time left in the day in which to try to quickly earn more money. Bank loans were out of the question, as was the prospect of trying to borrow money from her other family members. I decided I needed to help this woman. I had grown to care a great deal about her and could not stand by and watch her family be dissolved.

I talked it over with my parents and my husband; we decided to try to raise the money for Lupe as a Christmas surprise. My father composed a letter that we could send out to family and friends. In the letter we described Lupe and her situation and asked for a ten-dollar donation. I gave copies of the letter to the parents of the children at my day care center and asked them to spread the word, too.

My first attempt at collecting money was with my weekly women's card group. They donated all of their winnings from that night and I came home with sixty-nine dollars. I was quite pleased with my first efforts at fund-raising and began to think that we just might be able to do this for Lupe after all.

I opened an account for The Children's Fund (as we named it) at my local bank and watched with pleasure as the money began to come in. In fairly short order we had received $1,200, almost a third of what we had set out to raise. A surprising setback arrived just as quickly, however: When the bank found out that The Children's Fund was for charitable purposes, they immediately closed my account. Stinging from this uncharitable act, I spent more than a week driving from bank to bank in an effort to find one that would take the money for Lupe's children. All this time I was getting checks in the mail every day. Even though we had only asked for $10 donations, I opened envelope after envelope containing $50, $200, or more. Neighbors were telling neighbors, my day care parents told their children's grandparents, and the whole effort snowballed.

The letters of support and goodwill that were folded around the checks were heartwarming. Many came from folks I did not know, and many of them told moving tales of their own immigrant forebears' arrival into the United States under somewhat less than legal circumstances. Despite the atmosphere of immigrant-bashing that reigned that election year in California, these strangers were opening their hearts and their wallets to an unknown Mexican woman. I knew that the holidays were a difficult time financially for many families, and yet here they were sending money to take care of the children of a stranger.

With Christmas only a week away, I was $850 short of the goal. The next day I received a check for $500 from a family who had decided to give all the Christmas money they'd received from their grandparents to Lupe and her children instead. A few smaller checks arrived to bring us closer to our goal, but we were still a bit shy of it. "A miracle," I told my next door neighbor, "that's what I need." And then the very next day, on Christmas Eve, one of my day care parents gave me a check for $200. In a little more than a month we'd raised the entire $3,900. The fines would be paid; the children could become U.S. citizens.

On Christmas Day my neighbor Gia invited Lupe, her children, and my whole family over for dinner. Some of the other neighbors and a few good friends joined us for the tearful moment when my husband and I presented her with a check for $3,900. Champagne flowed, and hugs were given freely.

There will soon be six proud new citizens of the United States. I will always remember the love, concern, and generosity of many people who helped this one family in need. Raising this money and seeing the look on Lupe's face and the happiness in her children's eyes meant more to me than any gift I have ever received. It truly is more blessed to give than to receive.

—CATHY CALDWELL
Rocklin, California

First Christmas

 Y HUSBAND, MATT, AND I had been married only two months, and our first Christmas together was approaching. It was also my first Christmas away from my family, which I knew would be difficult. I had always loved being with all my brothers and sisters during the holidays, and my mom had always made the season joyful with her traditional parties, wonderful cooking, and the excitement of dozens of beautifully wrapped gifts under the tree. She also had a special way of impressing on our family the deeper meaning behind our holiday celebrations, from the picture up on her bookshelf of Santa kneeling beside the Christ Child, to our Christmas Eve tradition of buying and secretly delivering gifts to a needy family. From her example, I have known since I was a young child that Christmas represents something very special.

And so, now that I was beginning my own little family, I wanted to create some of those same warm traditions and memories that reminded me of the real significance ot the season, even if I was three thousand miles away from home. I had heard that my church, which puts on an outdoor living Nativity scene every year, was looking for volunteers to play the parts of Mary and Joseph. It was a tradition in the Washington, D.C., area where we lived, and I thought it would be wonderful to participate. So without even mentioning it to Matt, I signed up for both of us.

Matt is not a "performer," so to him the idea of being front and center stage as Joseph was a little unsettling. He had two main worries, he told me as we drove to the church that night: He was worried that he might have to say some lines during the enactment, and he was concerned that the church might not supply outdoor heaters!

When we pulled up to the church, we saw another couple who were just wrapping up their two-hour shift portraying Joseph and Mary. We were told that there was a ten-minute recorded tape that told the story, which repeated itself over and over. There was no speaking part for the volunteers, just a little bit of acting required. The baby Jesus was played by a "Baby Tender Love" doll, wrapped in old blankets—the same ones, I was sure, that were used year after year. Joseph would pretend to talk with the wise men while Mary held the baby doll and rocked it back and forth.

A gentle woman found us and directed us to the costume room. She picked out our robes and sashes and gave us our instructions. "When the recording starts," she said, "listen to the words and just go along with the story." Simple enough. We were to acknowledge the shepherds and the wise men when the time came, and devote the rest of the time to holding and adoring the baby. I figured that by the end of the two hours, on the twelfth time through the routine, we would have it down.

I came out of the dressing room with a blue cloak around me that was also draped over my hair. Matt was wearing a worn brown robe and, a tattered sash and had a fake beard glued to his face. I tried to hide my laughter when I looked at him, but we both knew how ridiculous we looked to each other. Matt still seemed somewhat uncomfortable with the idea of getting up on the stage, especially in his extremely fake-looking beard, knowing that many of his family and friends were coming by to see us. Because I had roped him into this "performance," I was feeling a little guilty. But we joked with each other as we walked out, determined to make the best of it.

As we approached the stage area, I was amazed at how many people were in attendance that night. There must have been 500 or 600 visitors before the night was through, and I suddenly felt a little stiff with stage fright. About the third time through the routine, I saw Matt's mother in the back of the crowd, waving her arms to get our attention. I was sure Matt saw her, too, because he couldn't keep the nervous smile off his face. Each time Matt and I exchanged glances, we both wanted to laugh, but we tried hard to focus our attention on talking to the wise men and fussing over the baby.

It was about the sixth time through the vignette before I realized how cold it was that night—only about 35 degrees. I pulled the blankets closer around the doll's little body and head, as any concerned mother would. I was gazing down at the baby, and the thought suddenly entered my mind: I wonder if it was cold *that* night—the night the *real* Christ Child was born? I began reflecting on the story I had heard so many times throughout my life and I tried to visualize the real Mary—not just as a character in a story written in words that were hard to understand, but as a person, a woman, a mother. Mary, the beautiful young virgin…a mere girl, really, several years younger than myself, who nevertheless would hold center stage in this dramatic event in history that would change the world forever.

For a brief moment, I felt as though I slipped away into another time and place. I saw the dusty stable and the rough dirt floor, a tiny wrinkled face against the straw. I could smell the musty odor of hay and cattle and saw the silent stabled animals, powerless to utter the sacredness they had witnessed. I looked over at my beloved husband, a simple carpenter, the only one who would hold my hand and wipe my brow…and give me an innkeeper's cool linen when the ordeal was over. And I saw the light streaming down from heaven, bursting through the slats of a crude stable, blending with the glow already radiating from a tiny, holy face. For that moment, I was no longer playing a part in a pageant. For one breathtaking moment, I *was* Mary, and I knew the tender emotions of her heart that wondrous night. As I embraced the baby against my chest, my heart swelled with a feeling I can only describe as pure love, and in that instant I knew that this child—God's own Son, the Savior of the world—also loved me. My eyes filled with tears of joy and gratitude for the warmth of His redeeming love.

Then I lowered my eyes to the crowd below and noticed a middle-aged woman who was standing alone, watching me closely, and she was weeping. Our eyes met, and then our souls touched, and we knew each other's thoughts. We were both reflecting on the woman Mary and what she must have been feeling that silent, holy night. Did she worry about the inadequate surroundings, or long to have the experienced hand of her own mother near during labor? Would she be prepared to raise this special child to fulfill his mission on earth, teaching him the tenderness and compassion he would need his entire life? When she looked into the smiling eyes of this new infant son, could she possibly know the pain and sorrow that would fill those eyes one day? Did she fear loving this child too much, knowing that her heart would break if he were ever taken away from her? Mary was the most "highly favored," chosen and blessed among women, but these were the concerns of a mother. Any mother.

As the woman and I looked deep into each other's hearts that night, we understood. Two people who had never met, and would never see each other again, had connected as women and as mothers—she, most likely a mother of children who had already left home, and me, a mother of a son to be born some months later.

I would never view Christmas quite the same way again. Although I would still enjoy the tinsel and wrapping, the decorated trees and the music, I would always remember that Christmas began with just a small family...far from home...and the love of a baby. I had felt for myself the real significance of Christmas. I knew my mother would be proud.

—KRISTEN GURKSNIS
Dallas, Texas

My Christmas Angel

N A COLD AND SNOWY DECEMBER MORNING in 1971, as I waited in front of the Children's Hospital for two of my Montreal Expo teammates, I felt slight twinges of nervousness and even some fear about the experience I was about to have. As a father of three healthy, happy children, it had always been difficult for me to see little ones suffering severe illnesses and disabilities.

Just as I concluded a short prayer asking that we would be able to leave something of value with the children we were to visit, Steve Renko, a big, strong, right-handed pitcher, walked up with a look of concern on his face. He was feeling the same things I was. A few moments later we were joined by Boots Day, a usually happy, but very tough little outfielder. He also expressed how these visits pained him. This would be a bit different from our normal visits, in that we were to spend it seeing children in the birth-defects wing. I had visited many children throughout my years in professional baseball (it's what we *did*—it was the *least* we could do) most of whom had been stricken with various illnesses such as cancer and heart defects, and several of these children had caused me to offer prayers of gratitude for my health and that of my family.

As Steve, Boots, and I were entering the hospital, we were immediately met by the most cheerful nurse I had ever seen. She literally bounced toward us exclaiming, "Oh, we're so glad you're here today. We love our Expos!" I wondered how someone who spent every day around sick and dying children could be so bubbly. As she led us through the hallways, we could hardly keep up with her as she was telling us how excited the children were to see us. That made me feel grossly inadequate and overrated. Just because we could play baseball and were well-known in Montreal—did that make us special? I thought not.

Finally we came to a large room and as we entered, I prayed that the shock and sadness I felt did not show through my forced smile. What we saw were about thirty young children with twisted, deformed bodies, some terminally ill, some destined to live a life of almost total helplessness. I swallowed hard and followed our perky little nurse into the room.

Usually we would visit for a moment or two with each child, sign a picture or baseball card, and leave them with some mementos from the team. But this time we were ushered to the front of the room and introduced to the children. As we were walking up, I noticed that the room was full of Christmas decorations and commented to the nurse how beautiful they were. She said, "The children made them." When I said I couldn't believe it, she replied, "Well, we helped, but they did a great job." She showed me a painting of Santa Claus that a little girl had painted with her foot because she had been born without arms. I was close to tears when I saw that little girl beam with pride.

After we were introduced, the nurse said, "All right, children, let's show our guests how much we appreciate them." For the next fifteen minutes these little children sang Christmas carols to us in both French and English. I was now feeling the tears welling up to the point where I knew I couldn't control them. Here we had come to cheer these sick little children and instead, we were being lifted by them. It was a moment I will always treasure. While they were singing, I noticed one child with a head twice the normal size for a five- or six-year-old. The veins were straining at her skin and, quite honestly, it looked grotesque. She had a condition called hydrocephalus (commonly known as water on the brain) and I pitied her with all my heart.

When the music was finished and we had answered some questions from the children, we began to go from bed to bed and personally visit each one. Recorded music played "Hark, the Herald Angels Sing" and "Silent Night" as we did so. Most of the children were pretty cheerful despite their conditions, but when I came to the bed of the little girl with the enlarged head, she wasn't smiling. I autographed a pictrure for her and kept my eyes on it instead of her. Finally, as I handed it to her and said, "Here you are, sweetheart— thank you for the beautiful music," she broke into a huge smile and looked straight into my eyes with the most loving gaze I had ever seen. She touched my hand and asked shyly, "Could you give me a kiss good-bye?" Her voice was angelic. Her eyes held mine, and were the most beautiful clear blue I had ever seen. I bent down and softly kissed her cheek as she gently clasped my hand. What had so recently seemed repulsive to me had somehow been transformed into exquisite beauty. My heart now knew what it was to love someone unconditionally, and I felt that same love coming from her.

I had kissed an angel at Christmastime, and the softness and tenderness of the moment I shared with her comes back to me every Christmas, to remind me that no matter what we look like, or how we are shaped, or what our living conditions are, we can still give the ultimate gift to others. The gift of love transcends all material riches, and this sweet little angel had given that gift to me to keep forever.

As the three of us left the hospital that day and went out into the freezing air, ice formed on our cheeks where the tears still streamed—tears from three grown men who, because of the warm spirits of a few small children, would never be the same again.

Sometime later, I realized the thing I had learned most from those children was simply this: They were born with limitations, but through their short, difficult lives, they had learned to concentrate on what they *could* do instead of what they *could not*. And nobody had told them they could not be happy. I now knew why that nurse was so cheerful. She was able to share that incredible love and the children's amazing accomplishments every day. Living and working with angels like these would raise anyone's capacity to love.

Merry Christmas, my little angel, wherever you are. I love you.

—RON BRAND
Los Angeles, California

The Story of Punkin and Boo

HIS IS A CHRISTMAS FAIRY TALE, with two good little girls and their
sweet little kittens, helpful strangers, and even a miracle or two. But
in fact it is not a fairy tale, as it all really did happen in Charlotte,
North Carolina, in the winter of 1988.

My two young daughters, Lori and Ellen (who are very big now but who
were then mere lasses of nine and eight) lived with their two kittens, Punkin and
Boo, in our neat little house in the suburbs of Charlotte. The girls loved their
kittens dearly and were hardly ever parted from them. Every night they tucked
their kitties in bed next to them, singing lullabies to soothe their kitty
nightmares and stroking them to keep their coats soft and shiny.

Like Lori and Ellen, Punkin and Boo were siblings, a brother and sister from
the same neighborhood litter. Punkin (as you might imagine from his name) was
orange, and Boo was a loving black kitten with a white dot on her nose, as
though it had been dipped in sweet cream.

One day—on Thanksgiving Day, as a matter of fact—while our family was
hard at work on the turkey dinner, the two kittens went out to play by
themselves in the yard. They were well-behaved kittens so they didn't stray far,
just over to the next yard to chase a squirrel or two or three. But those squirrels
ran out into traffic, and foolishly, the kittens did, too.

Within the space of just a few minutes both kittens had been hit by cars.
Thankfully, neither Lori nor Ellen saw this happen, but they learned the details

later from some young boys playing basketball nearby who saw the whole scene unfold.

Punkin was hit first. The driver did not stop to check the kitty's condition, but just drove on toward his important business. Then Boo was hit. The driver who ran over Boo was also in too big of a hurry to stop and check on a tiny kitten as it lay in the street. That's when the miracles began.

As the boys told Lori and Ellen, although neither driver stopped for the kittens, other drivers pulled over right away. First a young woman stopped, picked up Punkin's limp body, put him in her car, and left. Then another stranger stopped for Boo. The boys didn't know where either driver took the cats, but they were pretty sure that of the two, Boo was certainly dead—the woman who stopped for Boo had had to pick her little body up with a shovel.

My husband Doug and I told Lori that Boo was dead. She cried for two days straight. We launched a Christmas holiday search for Punkin, distributing flyers throughout the neighborhood and calling animal shelters to ask if he was there. When we came up empty-handed after searching all of the animal shelters in the area, we started to contact all of the veterinarians listed in the phone book. After several days of calling, we found him! He was somewhat battered and scarred, but otherwise in good health. The vet who had nursed him back to health wouldn't accept payment, and the Good Samaritan who loved animals enough to stop and pick Punkin up off the street and bring him in to the vet wouldn't accept the reward we offered.

And so from then on, Punkin would be the family cat, shared equally by the two girls now that Boo was gone. Lori and Ellen took turns sleeping with Punkin at night, but all three of them missed Boo.

What none of us knew was that of the two Good Samaritans who had stopped for our kitties on Thanksgiving Day, the second one was still working hard to bring Boo home.

I received a call one afternoon in mid-December from a woman who had seen one of the "Lost Kitty" flyers we had posted after the accident. "Thanks for calling," I said. "But we got our little orange kitty back. We found him at a vet's office." "Orange kitty?" the woman asked, sounding a bit confused. "No, I picked up a little black kitty in the street that day. She was pretty badly hurt but she is in better shape now. I've been trying to find her home for weeks, but I guess she's not yours. Sorry to have bothered you."

"A black kitty?" I asked quietly, not wanting to hope too much. "A black kitty with a little white spot on her nose?"

It was Boo! Boo with a shattered jaw, protruding shoulder, and mangled paw, but mighty happy to see us after all.

And so my fairy tale ends happily, with the good little girls and their sweet little kittens reunited by Christmas. My good little girls are in high school now, busy with homework and friends. But at Christmas every year I can still look into their bedrooms at night and remember the two little angels and their miracle kittens tucked into their warm beds, dreaming of sugarplums and catnip.

—MOLLY FURMAN
Charlotte, North Carolina

Exchange of Gifts

Y HUSBAND, JOHN, AND I had been blessed with three wonderful children and a happy life in the rolling hills of northern California. Throughout the early years of our marriage, I'd heard many stories about John's family, how they had come over to America many generations before, the impressive accomplishments of his forefathers, and wonderfully vivid tales of his own mother and father. It made for a rich family history. John took great pride in the book of Gallagher family history that his mother had written and published.

My own family story was not nearly as well documented. I knew a handful of colorful tales about my father, Wendell Thayer, and his rugged ranch life as a kid in a small eastern Oregon town, but he had died when I was fourteen. The tales had stopped, and I had long since lost track of that part of my family. Having three children of my own stirred up a sense that I should try to find out what I could about my family's history before the trail grew too cold. I didn't want my children to know only about one side of their faimily. As the year drew to a close and I geared up for my young family's Christmas, I resolved that I would spend time in the coming year trying to track down what I could. But where would I start?

Putting aside my thoughts of family roots, I threw myself into the Christmas celebrations. It is my favorite time of year. I love choosing just the right tree and hanging our family decorations. The house smells wonderful and I get that warm feeling of family, the advent of a truly blessed event, the continuity of generations, and the joy of remembering Christmases long ago.

My husband came home from the office one day in early December that year with a question for our youngest daughter: "Mary Beth, how would you like to fix up your old bike and give it to someone who could make good use of it?" Mary Beth had her eye on a new shiny yellow bike down at Dale's Schwinn Bike Shop. She was pretty sure that Santa would be dropping it off at her house Christmas morning, so she readily agreed to fix up her old purple bike to pass along to another child. One of the secretaries in my husband's office was divorced and having a rough time of it financially; her four-year-old daughter would be very happy to see Mary Beth's old bike under the tree that year.

But first, five years of bumps and bangs and rattles had to be smoothed away. Mary Beth and her dad cleaned up the bike with a little cleanser and polish. Then they rook it down to the Schwinn shop and had it serviced. They tinkered and oiled and spruced up the works, and then added a new seat, tires, and handlebar grips with plastic streamers. When it came home, it looked like a brand-new bike, ready to make any four-year-old happy.

A few days later the little girl's mother came to our house to pick up the bike. That is always an awkward situation; neither party feels quite comfortable. The recipient of the gift feels a bit shy about having to accept charity, and the giver of the gift feels a bit shy about being so fortunate that they can give things away. It is an unbalanced relationship that all too often dims the joy of the moment.

I invited her in. We adults oohed and aahed over the newly restored bicycle and agreed that it would be perfect for her daughter. Mary Beth peeked around a corner and waved at the woman, too embarrassed to come out and join us. To smooth over the moment, I relied on that old conversational standby, "So, are you from around here?"

No, no, she wasn't from around Santa Rosa, California, she told us. She was from a tiny little town in eastern Oregon, she said, so small that no one ever knew where it was. "What town?" I asked, as my ears pricked up. "Vale," she replied. "It is way up near the border with Idaho." I knew exactly where Vale was, it was the same tiny ranch town that my father had grown up in, on the ranch that my grandfather homesteaded!

I knew the stories of dusty roundups and slippery calves, of chuck wagons and hearty ranch breakfasts, all from those faraway days when my father was still alive and from two hazy trips to see Grandma when I was still a small child. It seemed so far away, like a black-and-white movie I couldn't quite tune in.

And that is how things were until that day just before Christmas twenty years ago. This young woman not only knew about the Thayer family; she could describe the big old boxy house my grandparents built and tell me exactly where it was! It was painted two different colors—one floor was a dusty brown and the other a deep pea-green—and it was built on the banks of the Malheur River. With her help we were able to go back to eastern Oregon the following summer, find the Hope Ranch, and get in touch with what few relatives I had in the area.

I don't remember her name, but this woman gave me a lovely gift that Christmas. What started out that day as an awkward charity encounter had turned into a wonderful afternoon of mutual gift giving. She was able to give her daughter an almost new purple bicycle with a banana seat, and I was able to give my children a part of their family history they would otherwise never have known.

—WENDY THAYER GALLAGHER
Santa Rosa, California

The Riches of Family

Y FATHER, WILLIAM KING DRIGGS, was a classical music teacher, and during the Great Depression music lessons were a luxury very few people could afford, so we were very poor in those days as my father struggled to keep students. We actually weren't poor; we just didn't have any money. But we always maintained that we had everything money couldn't buy. Besides having musical talent, my dad was a fine artist and writer, so our home was filled with music, with his beautiful paintings, and with many books.

Dad had taught each of his eight children to play a different musical instrument. We traveled every summer with our little family orchestra, giving concerts at churches and schools throughout the West. We didn't have too much on the table to eat and certainly no goodies or snacks in the icebox, but somehow we always managed some flowers and candles on the table. Our parents saw to it that we enjoyed the romantic atmosphere of gracious living even if we had very few of the practical necessities. You might say that in some ways we were truly rich.

Of course, Christmas was a big time for our family. But I remember one year we were so poor, we had to cut down the pepper tree in our backyard because we couldn't afford to buy a Christmas tree. Mother had always managed to put away a few dollars toward the big holiday and produced miracles of her own to surprise us, but this year was especially difficult. All the childhood diseases had struck our family—mumps, chicken pox, measles, and even scarlet fever. The doctor bills took away any Christmas money there might have been.

We had a family council to see if we could find a solution to our dilemma. Mother came up with an idea that we all accepted immediately. She would make her delicious "divinity" candy, which she was famous for, and put it in pretty little boxes, and Dad would paint some lovely watercolor pictures and hand-frame them. Then we would drive out to some busy boulevard on a Sunday afternoon and try to entice the drivers to stop long enough to buy our homemade gifts. The spot we chose to set up our business was the corner of Los Feliz Boulevard and Western Avenue on the border of Los Angeles and Hollywood. We leaned signs against our old Dodge touring car and went to work. That area was the "Sunset Boulevard" of the day: Cecil B. DeMille, Jack Dempsey, and other celebrities lived in the elegant neighborhood. All the more reason for us children to hate the idea of standing out there "hawking our wares." Of course, we would have done almost anything to ensure a happy Christmas, but the corner where we stood was very close to the city of Glendale where we lived, and I remember the agony of worrying that one of our friends might drive by and recognize us—even at the age of eight, I felt like I would die of embarrassment!

There was no magical ending to that episode. We stayed there all day in the southern California December heat—waving, flagging, yes, even singing songs and playing our instruments—and not *one* car or person stopped to buy one single item the entire day! We came home extremely discouraged, but still somehow managed to enjoy the beauty of the season, with the light from the candles on our little pepper tree and joyous Christmas music constantly filling our home.

That same Christmas remains clear to me because of another poignant memory. Each class in our elementary school had been assigned a needy family's name, and the children brought in canned goods and food items for a lovely basket for the family's Christmas dinner. I was as enthusiastic as the rest of the children about the project and contributed, too, although it was not easy to find anything in our pantry to spare.

A box was left on a classroom table for a couple of weeks for items to be deposited in, and I remember the feeling I'd get every time I noticed it getting fuller. I kept thinking of the family who might receive it—a family who would otherwise not have much of a Christmas dinner, who probably couldn't afford many presents or even a tree. During those weeks, I remember trying to visualize the family's reaction—their utter surprise and delight at the bounteous gift—and then their joy at being able to cook up a real "feast," with enough food to last a week! Because I was so consumed with the excitement of this little project, I gave very little thought to what I wanted for myself that Christmas. The true spirit of the season had created a warm feeling in my heart I hadn't experienced before.

The last day of school before Christmas I, along with a few other girls in my class, was asked to arrange the items in a huge basket and decorate it with a big bow and with some holly leaves and ornaments we had cut out of colored paper. That afternoon at home, just before supper, a lady came to our house and asked for my mother. When Mother came to the door, she beheld a beautiful basket of food, Christmas goodies, and even a turkey. As mother called all of us in to see the wonderful surprise, I immediately recognized every item in the basket, including my own decorations! My whole family was very touched by the anonymous gesture, but I burst into tears, devastated by the realization that some of my classmates would know that my family was the recipient of their charity. It was strange, but because of the intangible riches my family enjoyed, I had never considered myself poor, even though we really were—and suddenly the reality of our condition was very painful. That Christmas I had learned the lesson of the pure joy of giving, but I never dreamed I would also need to learn the important lesson of graciously receiving.

Year after year, Christmas after Christmas, our financial struggles continued, but my father refused to give up his dream of having a talented musical family of national fame. We lived out of a jelly jar full of the change that my parents brought home from the collection plate taken at the churches where we gave our little concerts. That jar was the only bank account we ever had. We seldom went to a denist, had no insurance, lived in rented houses, and wore hand-me-down clothes throughout our childhood. My father felt he was a miserable failure most of his life because he hadn't given his children any real security.

Remarkably, however, at the age of eighty, that same man, handsome still and revered by his entire family, stood straight and tall, leading his children and grandchildren in the family's theme song, "Love at Home," on national television for all to see. His lifelong dream of that little family orchestra becoming something quite remarkable had come true at long last. The fifty members of the "King Family" (which had sprung from his original eight children) had performed at a charity event some months before, where the head of ABC-TV had seen them and asked them to do a pilot for TV. The show struck a chord in the heart of America, and the family went on to have a weekly show for several seasons. My father passed away shortly after one of the early shows, but he died "with his boots on," doing what he loved more than anything in the world.

My family spent the next decade doing television shows and concert tours. We have many wonderful memories of the experiences of those years. But I recall during one of our Christmas shows watching the entire family gather around a twenty-foot-tall Christmas tree on the set of the TV studio. It was decorated with hundreds of lights and elegant gold and silver ornaments. The women were all dressed in white satin and the men were in handsome black tuxedos as we began to sing "The First Noel." And in my mind I suddenly recalled another picture of a younger family, gathering to sing the same song, but dressed in much simpler clothing, around a much smaller tree—a pepper tree. The scene was different, but the blend of voices and the feeling of peace and love was the same. My family's humble beginnings were made beautiful by loving and wise parents who taught their children that Christmas and its true meaning and message is a miracle in itself. My parents, who felt that they had given us so little, had bestowed on us the most priceless gifts of life—music, beauty, and the security that comes from family love.

—DONNA KING CONKLING
Roseville, California

The Silver Star

SHALL NEVER FORGET December 24, 1944, and the German prisoner of war who helped to make that night so memorable for me.

When the Allied forces made their big push into Germany, it was the duty of my military police battalion to take prisoners from the front lines into crudely constructed stockades. It was a bitter cold night and I found myself on duty helping to guard more than twelve hundred German prisoners. To say that the men in my battalion were a homesick bunch would be an understatement. The fact that it was Christmas Eve only added to our depression. One of our company, a man from the Smoky Mountains of Tennessee, stopped blowing on his hands long enough to say:

"What a cold, miserable Christmas! But just because we are stuck out here doesn't mean we can't do something about it. I'm going out to find a tree."

"Forget it!" another MP shouted. "There are no trees around here. Besides, we haven't anything to decorate with anyway."

Not to be discouraged, Smoky went into the darkness and later returned with a bedraggled specimen.

"You call that thing a tree?" our heckler continued. "In Texas we'd plow that under for a bush."

With determination and a positive attitude, Smoky began to decorate his tree with ornaments made from gum wrappers, candy wrappers, any scraps he could find. Several of the men not stationed directly at the stockade began to help our zealous friend with his seemingly impossible task. As we worked, I suddenly heard a voice calling from the stockade: "American! American!"

Turning toward the compound, I saw a German prisoner with one hand extended through the barbed wire. With his other hand he was motioning toward me. I quickly threw a shell into the chamber of my rifle and approached him with caution. What I saw in his hand astounded me.

This prisoner had made a beautiful silver star, entirely from gum wrapper foil, that was a work of art. Each of the points was long and straight and its three-dimensional form made it glisten in the moonlight. He placed the star in my hand and motioned to the top of our tree. Hoping he spoke some English, I said, "This star has such detail, are you a professional artist?" By his puzzled expression it was obvious he spoke no more English than I spoke German, so I took his contribution over and placed it atop our tree.

"Well, I'll be!" my heckler began again. "I hate to admit this, but that bush is beginning to look like a real tree. Guess I should have kept my mouth shut, eh, Smoky?" A loud cheer of agreement resounded from all the men. As we completed our tree, we began singing Christmas carols, and I noticed several of the prisoners joining in on "Silent Night." The last strains were fading into the night when I heard the same voice call, "American."

This time the prisoner had both hands extended through the barbed wire. Again I approached with caution, rifle ready, and again I was amazed at what he held in his hands. This German sculptor had made intricate figures of the Nativity scene—Joseph, Mary, and the Christ Child. He pointed under our tree as he handed me his exquisite, detailed work. I nodded my thanks and carefully placed the delicate figures where he had indicated.

As I reverently arranged the tiny figures made of sticks artistically covered with foil, the light from our fire actually seemed to give them a heavenly glow. I contemplated for a moment, in our wretched, war-torn condition, how far we had strayed from the love of that first Christmas night, and felt tears sting my eyes.

Looking at the stockade, I saw the prisoner behind the barbed wire, gazing out at our humble Christmas offering. I hurried back, smiled, and warmly shook his hand. He returned my smile and the firelight caught the tears that were in his eyes.

Since the close of World War II, I have thought often of this German prisoner of war and the tender feelings I had for him that night. Our meeting was brief; we were two ships that passed in the night, but we shared emotions that crossed the barriers of language and the devastation of war. I have always wondered what happened to him but somehow I know that, no matter where he is, he would agree that our only hope for lasting peace in the world is a return to the teachings of the tiny figure he so beautifully molded that cold December night.

—IVAN T. ANDERSON
Kaysville, Utah

A Glimpse of Christmas

T WAS ONLY SEVERAL DAYS UNTIL CHRISTMAS. My husband and I live in Venice, Italy, and we celebrate each day intimately, sweetly, with a thanksgiving that only people who have waited for each other seem to be able to sustain. We never wait for the calendar to drive our festivals. Still, it was my turn to program our Christmas journey—ten or twelve days to roam our beloved Umbrian hills, I thought. I sat in the *osteria* behind the ghetto, where I like to go sometimes to lunch on bread and soup, and to stay in the safety of old warm woods and soft light and the gentleness of the people who work and eat there.

The cook is named Giulia, and though she's lived thirty years in Venice, she still wears the imprint of the south, of her Calabrian blood and bones. She walks, generous flanks swinging easily, shoulders and neck brittle, carrying an invisible, ancestral water jug atop her head. At once an enchantress, an abbess, a goddess (who all do the same work, she says), Giulia believes in miracles. And on this particular afternoon, it was miracles about which she was convinced to talk. I'd come only for a bit of comfort and a place to think about my Christmas. She plunked down a liter-sized pitcher of Refosco, a fresh glass for me, one for herself, and I was fixed.

She opened by saying it is folly to ignore that myth and history and intelligence and hypothesis are inseparable, each being necessary to comprehend and embrace the others. There is great commodity in Giulia's security, able as she is to pull, willy-nilly, solutions, answers, from her stores of immutable truths. She is never bewildered. Nothing is illogical for Giulia except, perhaps, that one might seek to be free of pain. The only way, she says, to live without pain is to isolate, unloose one's self, so nothing will ever happen.

"A sort of blindness," I mused.

"Be careful," she said. "Don't confound the emotional death of a person with someone whose eyes don't work. I have a friend, Isabella, born in the village where I was born, who lives in Treviso. She has been blind for forty-six of her seventy-one years. She invites life in every moment, batting at it, willfully squeezing the joy and torment from it. She's the type who creates her own surprises. And she can see everything," Giulia said in her enchantress's voice. Inner sight, spiritual clarity, intensely heightened sensitivity—she spoke to these not uncommon traits of the blind, I thought.

"Yes, it's those," she conceded, "but also, on the past seven eves of Christmas, Isabella has been able to see, to open her eyes and see." I had no idea where we were heading. I poured more wine for myself. Giulia had yet to sip from her glass.

"The first time it happened," Giulia said, "Isabella was sitting, waiting for her daughter to come for her, to walk with her the twenty-five meters across the garden to the house where she lived. Together with her husband and their three adult children, they would share the traditional dinner of Christmas Eve there. She felt, heard, and then saw her daughter coming toward her—the daughter who was two when Isabella was blinded, the daughter who was then forty-eight years old. Was it illusion, a dream, a trick?"

Giulia continued to recount: "Isabella said nothing, touching her child's face and kissing her eyes as she did always. Her daughter felt the change. 'Mama, what is it? What's happened? Mama, Mama tell me,' she said."

"You are so beautiful," said Isabella to her daughter. Neither of them awake to anything but the moment, they walked to the other house, greeted the family, drank to their collective health and well-being. Isabella remained steady—no explosive announcements, no cries of sainted intervention. It was enough for her that it was happening. Isabella's granddaughter, daily companion to her since she was a baby, was then twenty-five, Isabella's own age the last time she was able to see. Isabella looked at her and saw the young woman who everyone had always said was in her image. She saw herself—herself as she had been—familiar, untouched, safe, as though time had neither thieved from nor redrawn her.

"Everyone seemed to understand, to accept," Giulia said, "that some sort of generous interlude was being shared by them." She said that no one—not Isabella, her daughter, or the children—doubted either that it was true or that it was ephemeral. No one raced to call a doctor or a priest. They were somehow prepared for it, anticipating it even as one might a shooting star, aware that its beauty was as precious as it was uncontainable.

No one expected that Isabella would wake the next morning still able to see. And she did not. The second and the third time on Christmas Eve that "the Graces came," as Giulia said in her abbess voice, the family began to think that some colloquy might be in order—some strike at understanding the event medically, physically. But Isabella was regularly examined, scrutinized by a team from the University at Padua. The physiological mechanism that permitted sight had been irretrievably destroyed. Still, the family brought their story to the university. The powers listened. Examinations, visiting doctors, probes, and theories were built and broken; there were no doubts that Isabella could not, would never, see.

Isabella continues to see. For a few hours, sometimes less, sometimes more, during the Vigilia, the celebration of the birth of Christ, Isabella sees. And no one who has ever known of these events has felt the need to sensationalize them or attach greater inferences to them. It's only that sometimes Isabella can see and that most of the time she cannot see. "Tranquillity with a thing so undecipherable is a gift of the southern mysticism," says Giulia. And we return to her comfort absolute in the face of the illogical.

"But what is she like—Isabella?" I ask of Giulia.

"She is tall and lovely with eyes unhaunted by their stillness," she says. "She lives with no fear. She laughs. She lives with no rage. She sees, tastes, smells, examines, caresses life as though it were ever on the edge of its moments. She is excited by music, by sun and rain, and the sound and smoke of her fire. She loves flowers and she loves bread. She eats cookies and drinks wine from the thin, etched goblets she drank from on her wedding day. She says memory is hunger. She says to live in the present is to be full.

"Her eyes are almost always full of tears, so much does she weep, does she ache for the beauty she feels and understands. *Sempre pieno di lacrime e briciole* [always full of tears and crumbs] is she, so that the first thing I do when I see her is to kiss the tears from her eyes and brush the crumbs from her breast," said Giulia in her goddess voice.

—MARLENA DE BLASI
Venice, Italy

The Good Samaritans

 SMILED HAPPILY to myself as I drove down the Colorado highway that afternoon, smiling in anticipation of seeing my family for a much-needed Christmas get-together. For two long years I'd been out of the country serving as a Peace Corps volunteer in Tonga, an island in the South Pacific, as one of the "Six Hundred Volunteers over Fifty," a program for older Americans. The scenery outside my car window was so different from the countryside I'd grown accustomed to; the dramatic snow-covered Rocky Mountains were a welcome sight.

My cheerfulness spilled over into friendliness toward my fellow mountain travelers—I had been playing "passing tag" with a U-Haul truck whose cab was filled with the excited faces of a father and his four young children on their way to a new home. We had become "freeway friends," smiling and waving at each other each time one of us pulled ahead.

It was their turn to lead as we came around the side of a mountain. The U-Haul truck was ahead of me in the same lane when it suddenly began to swerve and slip in the gravel on the side of the road. I watched as, in what seemed like slow motion, the truck flipped onto its side and slid backward toward my car, then, still on its side, slid out across the highway, across the median, and into the fast lane of oncoming traffic.

I remember reacting very calmly, pulling my car off the road, carefully removing the keys from the ignition and placing them on my seat, and then walking across the now-slowing lanes of traffic to reach their truck. The next thing I recall is standing in front of the truck windshield, now topsy-turvy on its side with four children pasted against the windshield and fire and smoke shooting out the exposed bottom of the truck. The children and their father were trapped inside and shouting for help. I started to try to kick the windshield in with my heavy leather snow boot, but soon realized that would not work. Suddenly a car full of college boys stopped to help. One of them climbed up the side of the truck to try to yank open the passenger door and lift the family out. I ran back to my car for blankets. As I did so, a woman ran toward me, waving and shouting, "Get those boys off the truck; it's going to blow!"

By the time I returned with the blankets, several other carloads of folks had stopped to help and a hammer and a fire extinguisher had been found. Some wise person shouted through the window to the children and told them to turn their faces away while we shattered the windshield with the hammer. The children were handed down one by one into the arms of waiting strangers. Four women now sat on the ground, each hugging a sobbing child wrapped in a blanket. One of the highway Samaritans, an off-duty paramedic, ministered to the nasty bump on the youngest child's head.

It was close to forty minutes before the ambulance and rescue squad reached our mountain location, but by then things were under control and none of the children seemed badly hurt. I was struck by the way so many had stopped to help, but when I mentioned it to one of the college boys, he just shrugged and said, "That's what it's all about, helping others."

I returned to my car after the family left in the ambulance and continued my drive toward the ski resort. Still calm and collected about what had happened, I wasn't really overcome by the drama of the incident until later on that afternoon when I heard it reported on the radio news. Then I began to shake uncontrollably and wonder aloud, "Why wasn't anyone hurt? Why wasn't the truck struck by oncoming traffic? Why didn't the truck blow up when the boys were crawling on top of it and the children were trapped inside? Why wasn't anyone hit by traffic when they stopped to help? Why wasn't anyone thrown from the vehicle as it careened across the road?" It truly was a Christmas miracle.

Actually, there is a bit more to this story that I'd like to tell. During my entire Peace Corps experience I had lived in a country where for the first time in my life, because of my white skin, I was a minority. For two years I experienced nothing but kindess, love, and acceptance. During that afternoon drive in the mountains and my playful waving friendship with my "freeway friends," I had begun to reflect on the troubled turn that race relations in America seemed to have taken in my absence. My children had sent me letters overseas describing the O. J. Simpson trial and the great wedge that it seemed to be driving between blacks and whites. You see, the family in the U-Haul truck was African-American.

But the minute that truck crashed on the freeway, I can say with great pride, not a single one of those cars filled with people who stopped paid one bit of attention to the color of the skin of those they were helping. This was a family in danger who needed immediate help, and those who responded were happy to give it. As I drove away from the scene of the crash, I felt a renewed sense of faith that Christmas truly shows the inherent goodness and love of the ordinary American.

—SUSIE WAGNER
Denver, Colorado

The Sacrifice

T HE YEAR WAS 1932 and the nation's economy was at an all-time low. The disastrous crash of 1929 had left its mark, and we were experiencing a time that was to become known as the Great Depression. I was in the eighth grade, and we all started school that fall with few clothes and school supplies. There was no lunch program, and for many students there was no food to bring. So those of us who could bring something to eat shared whatever we had.

I remember that whenever any of us had an extra penny, we would put it in an envelope and hide it. When we had twenty pennies saved, we would take them to the store and buy two cans of Vienna sausages, a treat far better than candy. Then we would find a secluded area, put all our lunches together, open the cans of sausage, and divide everything equally. Those were special days.

As Christmas approached that year, we didn't feel the excitement that usually comes with the holiday season. We understood about the Depression and knew there would be very little for any of us. But there was one desire we all had, though none of us would have mentioned it to our parents. A new sled had appeared on the market called the Flexible Flyer. With its sleek finish, sharp runners, and smooth handlebars that steered it easily and gracefully, it was the Rolls-Royce of all sleds.

We all marched to the hardware store one day after school to see the new wonder sled. "How much are the sleighs, Mr. Evans?" one of the boys asked.

"Well," he replied, "I think I can sell them for four dollars and ninety-eight cents." Our hearts sank. But that didn't stop us from dreaming the impossible dream.

School was finally dismissed for the holidays, and when Christmas Eve came, we had our usual Christmas play and party. We returned to our homes, happy, yet sad, feeling keenly the weight of those depressed times.

I awoke early Christmas morning but was not eager to get up. My mother finally called, so I dressed and we all went to the living room where the tree was. I was surprised to see that the tree had been redecorated and was more beautiful than ever. But the biggest surprise was still in store. There, underneath the tree, with a big red ribbon tied around it, was a shiny new sled—a Flexible Flyer!

I let out a startled cry and dropped to the floor, sliding my fingers along the satiny finish, moving the handlebars back and forth, and finally cradling the precious sled in my arms. Tears rolled down my cheeks as I looked up at my parents and asked, "Where did you get the money for it?"

My mother wiped away a tear with the corner of her apron and replied, "Surely you believe in Santa Claus. Open your other present."

I opened another box and there was a beautiful dress. I loved it, but my eyes were on the sled. I could only stand and gaze in awe. I was now the owner of a Flexible Flyer!

After our midday Christmas dinner, Mother announced, "Put on your boots and bundle up warm. We're going to town. We have another surprise for you." I didn't think anything could compare with the surprise I already had. Dad hitched up the team to our big sleigh, I loaded in my new sled, and we went to town. As soon as we crossed the bridge, I saw what the surprise was. Kids were everywhere, and so were Flexible Flyers. Main Street had been roped off so that we could start at the top of the hill and glide all the way down across the bridge without danger from cars. The entire community had turned out. Boys and girls were all jumping up and down, some were crying, most were throwing their arms around each other and shouting, "You got one, too!"

Our parents finally got us calmed down long enough to listen to instructions. Three farmers with their horses and sleighs would take turns pulling us to the top of the hill. The older boys went first, running and then flopping "belly first," as we called it, onto their sleds. We watched as they glided effortlessly over the crusted snow. Faster and faster they went, crossing the bridge and coming to rest amid the cheers and clapping of parents. We all took turns, and as the day wore on, we got braver and wilder. The boys discovered they could do tricks by dragging their feet in a certain way, causing their sleds to turn around and tip over. We all got caught up in this adventure, tumbling in a tangle of arms and legs, laughing helplessly as we slipped around, ending up in a pile of bundled bodies.

As night drew near, our parents called for us to stop—it was time to return home for chores. "No, no," we cried. "Please let us stay." Reluctantly they agreed, releasing us from chores for this one time only. When they returned it was dark, but the moon shone brightly, lighting the hill. The cold wind blew over our bodies; the stars seemed so brilliant and close, the hill dark and shadowy as we made our last run for the day. Cold and hungry, but happy, we loaded our Flexible Flyers and returned home with memories that would last a lifetime.

Everywhere I went in the days that followed, my Flexible Flyer went with me. One night I decided to go to the barn, as I often did, just to watch Dad at work. I noticed that one of the stalls was empty. "Where's Rosie?" I asked. "She isn't in her stall."

There was an awkward silence, and my dad finally replied, "We had to sell her. She cut her foot on the fence."

Sell Rosie? I thought. *Gentle, friendly Rosie?*

"But the cut would have healed," I said. "Why didn't you sell Meanie? She never does anything we want, but Rosie always leads the herd into the barn."

Dad didn't say anything, and suddenly I knew. Rosie had been sold to buy my Flexible Flyer. She was the best and would bring more money; and my parents had given the best they had—for me. I had always understood that my parents treasured me dearly, but until that moment I had never known a love so great. I ran from the barn in tears and hid myself behind the haystack.

I returned to the hill the next day and told my best friend about Rosie. "Yes, I know," she said. "My dad took ten bushels of apples from our cellar and took them to Pocatello and sold them door to door. He's never had to do that before. That's how I got my Flexible Flyer."

A growing amazement overtook me. "But how did they know?" I asked. "I didn't ask for a sled, so how did all the parents know we all wanted Flexible Flyers?"

Little by little we began to put the pieces together. Everyone had a similar story to tell. Then we began to realize how the entire community had united in one monumental effort of sharing, trading, peddling, extra working, and, most of all, caring, to buy the Flexible Flyers. None of us ever had the slightest hint of what was going on right under our noses. That had to be the best-kept secret of all time in so small a community.

When school resumed and we marched into our classroom and stood by our desks waiting for the teacher to say those familiar words, "You may be seated," it seemed we all stood just a bit taller. Not that we had grown in stature, but we had grown in a different way. Nothing had really changed. The economy was still the same and we still shared our lunches and saved our pennies for the sausages, but inside we had all changed. We were happier, we played harder, and we studied more diligently. It was as if we had all committed ourselves to be the best we could be, to make our parents and community proud of us. It was the only way we knew to say "thanks."

When the snow finally melted and it was time to store the sleds, we were reluctant to part with them. We clung to them as a child clings to a favorite blanket. They had given meaning to our lives and provided us with a sense of identity. That terrible monster, the Great Depression, no longer seemed such a threat to us. Somehow we knew there would be better times, a brighter tomorrow, and a more prosperous future.

Many years later, long after I married, I asked my mother how they had managed to keep that secret, and who started it. Her eyes twinkled. She gave me one of those warm, loving smiles that only a mother can give and replied, "My dear daughter, you must never stop believing in Santa Claus."

—ANEY B. CHATTERTON
Soda Springs, Idaho

A Miracle Touched My Life

ET ME TELL YOU ABOUT A MIRACLE that touched my life. On Election Day, 1988, I was seriously injured in an automobile accident. I had been out on an early Christmas shopping expedition with my friend Joyce Petriello. As we approached a busy intersection on Highway 85, a speeding car knocked us seventy-five feet into the median. Luckily, we had our seat belts fastened. Joyce was not too badly hurt—her wrist was broken and she was bruised—but I was more seriously injured. As the rescue workers pulled me from the car, I told them my neck hurt. After X rays were taken, the doctors told me why my neck hurt so badly: Two cervical vertebrae had been injured, one of them so badly that my injury was classified as a broken neck.

My sons, Ennis and Wink, had heard of a fellow named Dr. Allen McDonald who specialized in spinal injuries. After looking at my medical records, he agreed to take me on as a patient. On November 14, I underwent a complex medical procedure in which bone was taken from my pelvis for use in a graft to fuse the injured vertebrae. This procedure was followed by the required surgical repairs on my neck. The doctors discovered that my spinal cord was not severed, but it was badly damaged. The prognosis was that I would live as a quadriplegic, completely paralyzed from the neck down.

Long after the surgery, I relived the long ride to the operating room. It was big and cold and bright with light, like something out of those old Buck Rogers movies. Then a deep religious feeling overwhelmed me: I was in the valley and shadow of death. God was my Shepherd, and I knew that it was only by His grace that I would live and would walk again some day.

On November 23 the doctor held a medical conference with me, my two sons, and their wives, Laurien and Bonnie. He gave us a devastating report: I would leave his spinal center in a wheelchair, I would require round-the-clock care, and I could never live alone. This was not what we wanted or expected to hear, but the family support was strong. My accident had humbled us all and drawn us closer to each other and closer to God.

As the news spread about the grim prognosis, relatives and friends everywhere started to pray for me. Members of their churches and members of my church in Fayetteville and even the church of my childhood in East Point all joined in prayer vigils for me. This kind of Christian loving care changed my attitude for the better; until then I wasn't sure that I wanted to continue to live helplessly paralyzed from the neck down.

I could raise my elbows slightly but could not lower them. I promised God that if He would help me, I would do everything that my medical team and physical therapists asked of me to the best of my ability. I promised God I would work hard.

I was the oldest patient at the hospital. Most of the patients at Sheperd's Spinal Center were young people, eighteen to twenty-five years old. It was heartbreaking to see such fine young people condemned to helplessness.

To call a nurse I had to sip and puff and blow in a straw. To bathe me the nurses would put me into a fishnet stretched over a frame and hose me down. While I lay in bed, attendants turned me every two hours. I couldn't comb my hair, brush my teeth, or feed myself.

On the first of December, I wiggled my toes. My ability to move my toes was a sign of hope and the nurses and doctors all came to my room to congratulate me.

The week before Christmas my family came to the hospital and took special training on how to take care of me. My sons wanted me home for Christmas, even if only for a few days before returning to the hospital.

Just before my trip home for Christmas, there was a party at the hospital. The nurses wore reindeer costumes; the doctors wore Santa Claus suits. They all tried hard to create a holiday mood for the patients, but the party was a bittersweet experience. Some eighty patients in wheelchairs filled the room. I knew that few would be able to go home for Christmas like I would.

Yes, I did go home for Christmas that year. As my son carried me through the door into his house, he shouted, "Here I come with my Christmas present for all the family!" On Christmas Eve I went with my family to church, despite my reluctance to face the world from a wheelchair. When we sang my favorite carol, "Silent Night," in the candlelit church, I was glad I had come after all. I felt close to God, and knew that I needed to strengthen my faith and trust in Him to help me walk again.

On Christmas Day, seated at the dinner table surrounded by the family I love, I was able to remove the leather straps that held utensils in my hands and eat without their aid. It was an incredible step in the right direction.

It was months later that I finally left the Sheperd's Spinal Center. On February 22, 1989, I stood alone with no cane and said good-bye to the staff and the other patients.

I praise God every day when I get our of bed and put my feet on the floor and walk. Not only did He hear my prayers, but He heard the prayers of all of the friends and relatives who prayed for me. Only one in a million quadriplegics is ever able to walk again, but I believe that I am a true testimony to the fact that God hears and heals when we pray and believe.

—MARIANNA SHUGART LANEY
Fayetteville, Georgia

Someone to Watch Over Me

 BELIEVE IN ANGELS. Angels in heaven and angels on earth. I have been richly blessed to have three angels in my life, all of them men: my husband Michael, my priest Father Foley, and Fernie. Let me start with Michael.

In the summer of 1980, Michael and I were married by my lifelong friend and priest, Father Foley. Michael had a job with the Boulder Police Department, we soon had two sons, and life was good. We struggled to make ends meet as most young couples do; I had some medical bills due to a kidney problem, and we had the additional expense of Michael's flying lessons. Michael had grown up the son of an airline pilot, he had two brothers who were pilots, and flying just seemed to be in his blood. He continued his lessons for four years and finally became an instructor. All the money we had put into flying was going to be worth it someday when he got a job with the airlines.

Then in October 1990, the police came to my door one night to tell me that Michael had been killed in a plane crash. My world was shattered. For weeks, all I could do was cry. The hardest moment of my life was when I had to tell my two little boys, just two and four years old at the time, that Daddy wouldn't be coming home anymore. During those first months of overwhelming grief, my dear friend Father Foley would call weekly from Baltimore to check on me. I told him that Tommy and Ryan kept asking where heaven was and if they could go there to visit Daddy, and I said that I had no answers for them, only more tears. Father Foley gently offered a solution: "Tell them that Daddy went to heaven because Jesus needed someone to teach the new angels how to fly." It was, of course, the perfect answer, and it finally gave the boys peace. Father Foley also reminded me that all things happen for a reason, and that someday I would understand why Michael had died.

Our first Christmas without Michael was approaching and I was still numb. We had had company ever since the funeral, and someone from Michael's family or mine had been staying with us every day for the past six weeks to help with the boys and be of comfort to me. On top of everything else, there had been a recent homicide in our town and I was afraid of being alone.

A week or two before Christmas, my first night alone with the boys in our house, I received my miracle. I couldn't go to sleep that night—I felt so alone and so afraid. Tommy and Ryan had been sleeping with me ever since Michael died, and although the three of us were trying to pull together, the pain was still unbearable. That particular night I was haunted by thoughts ot Micheal's death, wondering how long he had lived after the crash while the police searched for him in the mountains. I wondered where he was now—if he was okay—and if he missed us as much as we missed him. I guess I finally cried myself to sleep.

At about four in the morning something woke me up. I opened my eyes to a very bright light and saw a figure standing at the foot of my bed. The figure was brilliant beyond description and seemed almost transparent. Although the facial features were hard to distinguish, I immediately knew it was Michael. I sat up in bed and kept rubbing my eyes, thinking I was dreaming. But even more incredible than what I saw in front of me was the overpowering feeling of love—an inexpressible sweetness—that filled the room. Without words, the angel spoke to my heart, letting me know that he was okay, that he was in a wonderful place, and that we would be okay, too. He told me how much he loved us and that I shouldn't be afraid because he would be watching over us, protecting us. As I started to tell him how much we loved and missed him, my little Tommy woke up. He sat up in bed and pointed at the figure in front of us and said, "Mommy, is that my daddy? Yes, that's my daddy." Tommy and I hugged and cried and then very peacefully went back to sleep. I was no longer afraid to be alone. When Christmas came, I knew I had received a very special gift from God: the knowledge that Michael was watching over us and that we would all meet again someday.

The next few years were extremely difficult and at times I wondered if God had forgotten me. My beautiful mother, who had been my greatest support, died of cancer. My kidney condition was getting worse and I was told I would evenrually need a transplant. And I needed help raising my two sons. I was only thirty-one and knew I would someday want to remarry if I could only find someone who would love my children as their own. Father Foley continued his support for me through those years, and always counseled me to pray to find such a companion, along with praying for a solution to my kidney problem. I followed his wise advice and prayed daily for those things.

I met Fernie at my bowling league. We were just friends at first, but after dating for about a year, I knew I loved him. He was wonderful to my boys, and together, we were able to start laughing again. We shared everything with each other—everything, that is, except my one secret: my need for a kidney transplant. I was getting sicker and sicker and I was afraid that if he knew the extent of my condition, he might not want to share in that burden—the cost, the months of recovery, the potential dangers. Two weeks after I finally got up the nerve to tell him, Fernie proposed to me. He wanted to share his life with me despite the hardships. I knew my prayers had been answered. Father Foley was there to marry us, and Tommy and Ryan, now five and seven, couldn't wait to start calling him "Daddy."

We hadn't even been married two years when I received the bad news: I needed a kidney transplant immediately. Although I was heartsick, the doctors told me that between my five brothers and sisters, I should be able to find a donor who would match my blood and tissue type. My blood was A positive and anyone with type A or O could be a possible match, provided they had the same tissue type. My wonderful brother Dave told me he'd give me *two* kidneys if I needed them, but when he went down to be tested, found out his blood was B positive. As it turned out, all my siblings had the wrong blood type except one brother, who unfortunately had only one kidney.

Fernie knew how upset and afraid I was, and with great tenderness said, "Honey, I have A positive blood—I'll give you a kidney." We both knew the odds of his tissue being a match and lightly dismissed the thought, until I went to the hospital for tests. When they asked me if I had a donor and I jokingly told them my husband was willing, they decided to test him. Our blood was mixed together to see if there was any rejection factor, and amazingly, we were a perfect match—blood *and* tissue type. My husband, my hero, was willing to go through this extremely dangerous and painful procedure to make me whole again. Somehow I knew God and Michael were still up there together working miracles for me, and they had sent me Fernie.

Of the 665 kidney transplants performed at Presbyterian St. Luke's Hospital, none had been done between a husband and wife. It simply doesn't happen. Ours was their first, and it was a complete success. We were released in less than a week, and six weeks later, we enjoyed the best Christmas ever. We were a family now, healthy and happy, blessed by many miracles. I had believed our angel when, a few Christmases before, he had so lovingly assured us we would be okay, but I never dreamed that the two greatest desires of my heart would be provided by one remarkable man. I will be forever grateful, and I will continue to watch for angels.

—Dianne Campbell-Ostdiek
Lafayette, Colorado

～ *Acknowledgments* ～

OUR WARMEST THANKS TO the *real* "miracle workers" at William Morrow, especially Senior Editor Toni Sciarra and Assistant Editor Katharine Cluverius, and our extraordinary agent, Sheree Bykofsky.

Our deep gratitude to all of the following people: Bill Adler, Jr., Xan Albright, Jettie Jacob and Ivan T. Anderson, Barbara Arfsten, Scott and Lindsey Arfsten, Kerstin Backman, the Basye family, George Bingham, Ross and Diane Bjella, Marlena de Blasi, Daryl Bohnstedt, Ron and Candy Brand, Lori Buher, Yvonne and Bill Burch, Katherine Burns, Anne Burt, Margaret Cable, Cathy Caldwell, Dianne Campbell-Ostdiek, Aney B. Chatterton, Jane Clayson, Chris Conkling, Jim and Donna Conkling, Brooke Cowan, Delys Waite Cowles, Chuck and Barbara Curtis, Holly DeGroot, Virginia Dolar, Ben and Nancy Dominitz, John Emery, Diana Griego Erwin, Pete and Joan Fellows, Molly Furman and the Furman family, Wendy Thayer Gallagher, Jannis Gardner, Kit Dillon Givas, Stanley Glassover and the rest of the Glassover family, Dr. Bruce Goldberg, Linda Grimes, Gayle Groberg, Vivian Gundestrup, Kristen Gurksnis, Mark Victor Hansen, Pat Huber, Inez Humphries, Rabbi Abie Ingber, Mary Kelly, Sally Kuch, Rahima Kupper, Marianna Shugart Laney, Miki Hsu Leavey, Pete Lewis, Nora Lynn, MarGene B. Lyon, Raynier Maharaj, Gary McCann, Isaiah McKinnon, Elisabeth McPhail, Frank G. Miller, Michael Miller, Sherry Miller, Vicki Mitchell, Allyson Moring, Robin Montgomery, Karen Morrow, Tonya Morrow, Laura Mulrooney, the Northam family, Cathe Odom, Sabine Painter, Dr. Helen Pensanti, Jenn Pfeiffer, Olivia Pratt, Louise Reardon, *Reader's Digest*, Carla Rey, Valerie J. Reynoso, Mary Jane Rhodes, Mary Beth Gallagher Salmon, Peter Sander, Rev. Howard C. Schade, Sandi Schureman, Beverly

Shaver, Cynthia Stewart-Copier, Cathleen Swanson, Jeanne Tate, Kelly Strong Thacker, Jan Tilmon, Christopher J. Trujillo, Nancy Trythall, Susie Wagner, Marian Jeppson Walker, Teresa Walker, Laurette Walton, Todd Walton, Bonnie Williamson, and Velora Wells.